Killed In Camelot

Robert Kennedy, MCA, the Mafia, and the Death of Marilyn Monroe

By Eric Jensen

Table of Contents

Introduction

In the summer of 1962 rumors of a Marilyn Monroe and Robert Kennedy affair where spreading through Hollywood. When Marilyn asked her friend and masseur if he had heard the rumors he replied "all Hollywood was talking about it." On the day before Monroe's death those rumors finally made their way into print in a Dorothy Kilgallen gossip column. In that column Kilgallen also mentioned a scandalous photo of Marilyn. The weekend before her death, Marilyn and her companion, Pat Kennedy Lawford were visiting Frank Sinatra's Cal-Neva lodge. According to photographer William Woodfield, a photo of Marilyn was taken that weekend that included Chicago mob boss Sam Giancana. FBI agent, Bill Roemer confirms Giancana was there.

According to Shirley MacLaine, Hollywood was entertaining another MM/RFK rumor during that fateful summer. The basis of this one was that Robert Kennedy and the Justice Department were going after the powerful media conglomerate MCA on behalf of Monroe. At the end of 1961 a grand jury was convened in Los Angeles to determine if MCA was involved in a conspiracy to monopolize the entertainment industry. Civil and criminal charges were expected. This was precisely the same time period that Marilyn first met RFK and also when she fired MCA as the talent agency that represented her. In over 50 years and 100's of books about Marilyn Monroe's life and death, the connection between these interrelated circumstances are barely even mentioned. This book sets out to change that. In the weeks and days before her death, Monroe was reaching out and trying to contact Robert Kennedy. This book attempts to show that it had nothing to do with an actual affair between the two but it had everything to do with the mistaken gossip that there was an affair. Circumstances in the MCA case had deteriorated to a point where Marilyn had to feel she was going to be blamed for what was happening in

Hollywood. In mid July 1962, the Justice Department announced it was going forward with it's case against MCA. MCA's talent agency represented between 60 and 70 percent of Hollywood's best talent. Just two weeks before Monroe's death the company was forced to dissolve their agency, leaving these actors without representation. Given the rumors that were circulating, I'm sure Marilyn wanted to set the record straight that she had nothing to do with this case. The men that ran MCA were powerful enough to make or break careers. It was also well known that both the president and chairman of the board of MCA were mob connected.

The weekend of her death Monroe was trying to contact her old publicist Rupert Allan, and also George Barris, who was working on her biography. Isn't it likely she wanted to tell her side of the story about the Cal-Neva photo and the MCA case. After her death this was turned into a press conference where she was going to expose her affairs with the President and Attorney General. While that was complete nonsense it was built upon a kernel of truth.

This book attempts for the first time to separate the kernels of truth from the countless lies, misrepresentations, misinterpretations and misinformation that has circulated for over a half a century. It does this by the construction of three new scenarios that incorporate new evidence and analysis into Monroe's death. A scenario is constructed for each possibility; suicide, accident and murder, allowing the reader to reach their own conclusions. Marilyn Monroe died from an oral ingestion of drugs, not from an injection, suppository or enema. If the drugs were dissolved in a liquid and given to Monroe by someone she trusted, it could still be murder. The final chapter of this book names a person who had the means, motive and opportunity to kill Marilyn Monroe. It's a name that's sure to surprise you. This person is still alive and it's high time she finally revealed what happened on August 4, 1962.

My goal in writing this book is to make a major contribution towards helping unravel the mystery that surrounds the death of Marilyn Monroe. The reasons I'm writing this are twofold. First, I think the memory of Monroe deserves better than the lies and mistakes that masquerade as fact, and second, history deserves better. Especially the history surrounding the assassination of John F. Kennedy. Kennedy's death may have been nothing less than an overthrow of the government, a coup d'etat in the USA. It's imperative for Americans to sort this history out. As of the beginning of 2018, all the government records dealing with the assassination of JFK have not been released. There's still hope to bring clarity to the greatest mystery of the 20th century. Was Lee Harvey Oswald solely responsible, or was there a greater conspiracy involved in the murder of an American president. While that question to date hasn't been definitively answered, there can be no doubt that there was a conspiracy to cover up the circumstances that surrounded Kennedy's death that reached into the highest levels of government intelligence agencies. Part of that cover-up involved the dissemination of "red herring" leads and documents designed to muddy the waters and lead investigators away from the truth. It's a legitimate question to ask if the same thing happened concerning the death of Marilyn Monroe.

There are many similarities and correlations involved in these two deaths. The same macro political events and tensions shaped how the stories would later be told. The same scandals and controversies provide fertile ground for all manner of conspiracy theories. With only fifteen months separating the deaths of Monroe and Kennedy, they occurred in roughly the same time period. Many of the same characters played a part in the buildup to their deaths, and it's likely both of their lives were effected by the strange interplay of the CIA and the Mob in the assassination plans for Fidel Castro. Monroe's death has become a subset of JFK's death. Her name regularly appears when authors speak of Kennedy's infidelities and her connection to Frank Sinatra brings her into stories centering around Sinatra and Sam Giancana, boss of the Chicago "Outfit." The connection became cemented when it became clear that Monroe crossed paths with Sam Giancana the weekend before her death at the Cal-

Neva casino and resort. There is a reliable source, retired FBI agent Bill Roemer, who says Giancana was there that weekend. Unfortunately, he is the same source for many of the ugly rumors and lies that have sprung forth about that weekend. Many authors repeat his claims that Monroe and Giancana had sex that weekend without ever including the fact that Roemer himself was just making an assumption based on information he was piecing together. He was listening to a bugged conversation and couldn't make out everything that was said. He really wasn't totally sure who Giancana and his fellow mobster were talking about. He admitted that he was piecing bits of the conversation together and when he heard something that was said about Giancana having sex with the "same broad" as the Kennedys, he just assumed it was Marilyn. We don't know the context of the conversation. We don't really know what Giancana said before his cronies comment, he could have been joking, lying or talking about Kennedy paramour Judith Campbell. Indeed it seems many of the elements of the JFK/Campbell/Giancana connection have been grafted onto Monroe's story. Because of Roemer's baseless testimony and rumors of photographs taken that weekend, it's assumed to be a fact that Giancana had sex with Marilyn Monroe. This has led many credible authors to write things like Monroe regularly "cavorted with gangsters." This simply isn't true. I've read credible assassination researchers also repeat, as fact, that Monroe was a friend of Johnny Rosselli. Some go as far as a ridiculous assertion that Monroe was Rosselli's occasional girlfriend!

In 2007, the CIA confirmed what many historians and researchers had known for decades. Giancana and Rosselli, both known and notorious gangsters, were hired by the CIA to assassinate Cuba's leader, Fidel Castro. For any future researchers out there that want their reconstructions of history to be accurate, allow me to set the record straight about Monroe's involvement in the doubtful "Double Cross" theory. There's no evidence that Monroe ever said two words to Rosselli. It's likely she knew of him, but any kind of sexual relationship with Rosselli (or Giancana, or ANY mobster) is simply absurd.

During her life, Monroe would recall fondly listening to Joe Schenck tell stories of early Hollywood. Before he ever met Marilyn, Schenck ended up, along with Rosselli, going to jail because of the Willie Bioff scandal, the mobs shakedown of Hollywood studios in the 1930's. Schenck was found guilty of tax evasion for his involvement in paying off the mob. He turned government witness and gave information that helped send Rosselli to jail. After they were all released I think it's likely Schneck would have warned a young Marilyn to stay away from "Handsome Johnny." Up until the Cal-Neva weekend, the closest any Marilyn biographer has come to linking Rosselli to Marilyn is by saying Rosselli used to pick up his girlfriend after she played card games at Marilyn's boyfriend's mothers house. From that paltry connection, stories of a friendship have sprung, and now she has become his occasional girlfriend! These lies and countless others are among the reasons why I feel Monroe deserves better.

What DID happen at Cal-Neva? This is just one of the areas that this book will be exploring. What happened that weekend is a crucial set-up for how Marilyn's final week played out. While the events of this weekend are important, for an understanding of Monroe's death, nothing is more important than her relationship with Robert F. Kennedy. Over half the book is dedicated to explaining Marilyn's connection to RFK and the entire Kennedy family. For over half a century, a Monroe/RFK affair is the cornerstone on which all conspiracy theories have been built. My intention is to show that BOTH the efforts to reveal this rumored "affair" and the efforts to deny it, have been the smokescreen that has obscured the truth about what really happened.

Far more important than sex is the possibility that RFK was using Marilyn for other reasons, and these reasons have been inexplicably ignored. Chances are you never heard about the government's antitrust lawsuit against MCA. So you may be surprised when I tell you that this case was instrumental in Marilyn's death. The clues have been there for decades, yet no one has realized their importance. In the mid 1990's, Susan Strasberg's book included a quote from Ralph Roberts (Marilyn's masseur) who was relating a conversation he had with Marilyn shortly before her death. What's interesting about this quote is that almost all biographers and conspiracy theorists use parts of it, yet no one else besides Strasberg includes the most important part. Conspiracy theorists use the first part which has Marilyn asking Roberts if he has heard the rumors of a Monroe/RFK affair. He replies that all of Hollywood is talking of nothing else. This is used as evidence of an affair. Other biographers, attempting to prove there was no affair, offer up Marilyn's response of "he's not my type, or "he's too puny" as evidence that there was no affair. Almost everyone fails to include the last line, which is the most relevant part. Strasberg's account of the exchange includes the most important line. Here's how it reads in her book, *Marilyn and Me*: (Ralph Roberts is speaking) "She asked me if I'd heard the rumors about Bobby and her. She said, 'It isn't true. Anyway, he's so puny. Bobby is trying to break up

MCA and he asked me to help him.' She loved helping to do something like that."

   In Marilyn research it's important not to put too much faith in one witness or a single quote. You should always try to verify with multiple attestation. So what are the facts about Monroe and MCA? We know that Marilyn signed on with the talent agency MCA about the same time she established her production company. There's abundant information on previous agents like Johnny Hyde and Charles Feldman, but it is difficult to find any information on why Marilyn decided to leave MCA at the end of 1961. What we do find on closer examination is two more sources that claim it might have had something to do with Robert Kennedy. We'll examine those sources more in Part II of this book. I think it's a very important, and an untapped episode in Marilyn's last year that provides valuable clues in the investigation of her death. It's actually one of seven key areas of interest that provide clarity on what exactly happened on Marilyn's last day alive. There is a vast amount of information and misinformation involved in an investigation into Marilyn's death. Much of it is just unimportant noise that obscures what's truly relevant. I've tried to narrow the scope of this investigation to seven key areas.

The seven "keys" necessary to finally unlock the mystery of Marilyn Monroe's death are:

1. The Kennedy Connection

2. Lesbian Rumors

3. MCA Lawsuit

4. The Cal-Neva Weekend

5. RFK's Movie

6. Marilyn's Publicists

7. Prescription Drugs

We've already touched on three of the seven "keys." Her connection to the Kennedy family, the weekend at Cal-Neva and the MCA investigation.

The other keys to unlocking the mystery involve investigating these topics; rumors that Marilyn "dabbled in lesbianism" towards the end of her life, RFK's movie *The Enemy Within*, Marilyn's relationship with her publicists Rupert Allan and Pat Newcomb, and finally the question of, "Where did the drugs come from that killed Marilyn Monroe?"

An investigation into those seven key areas yields all the clues necessary to unlock many of the mysteries that still surround Marilyn's demise. I want to warn you from the beginning, it's a work in progress, it's not a "case closed" type of work that provides a definitive answer. It's more of a call to reopen the investigation, or maybe more accurately, rethink about what actually what happened. This book WILL provide valuable new evidence that will make you re-think everything you've ever believed about Marilyn's death.

Occam's razor is a problem solving principle where you attempt to use the fewest amount of assumptions possible, and explain phenomenon with the simplest explanation possible. It's very to difficult to apply Occam's razor to the death of Marilyn Monroe. There is no simple explanation that can explain the contradictory mess that results from an investigation into Marilyn's death. They only thing clear about this case is that an incredible number of people are lying. The amount of lies and contradictions can make your head spin. So not only does any scenario have to explain the facts in a way that's scientifically sound, the theory also has to explain who's lying and why. It has to explain the behavior of all the people involved. An additional consideration is the fact that many of the major players involved refuse to disclose ANY pertinent information. An investigation into Marilyn's death leads to a lot of questions. Why did the housekeeper change her story? Why did the doctors lie about the timeline and why didn't they disclose important information concerning Marilyn's prescriptions? Why didn't Frank Sinatra or Pat Kennedy Lawford ever disclose what happened at Cal-Neva? Why has Pat Newcomb remained silent while her friends name has been tarnished and dragged through the gutter?

Why was there no formal investigation by the police? Why was there no coroner's inquest? Why did organs and tissue samples disappear from the morgue? Why weren't all of Marilyn's August phone calls ever released? These are not simple questions to answer without making a whole bunch of assumptions. Many people have given up trying. I'm not one of them. Many others say to just forget it and let the poor woman rest in peace. I can't do that either. What if her spirit can't rest until the truth is told? I believe Marilyn was denied justice and the great irony is that's it's because she had a relationship with a man whose sole job and responsibility was to uphold justice across the entire United States. There is no credible explanation as to why an official investigation or coroner's inquest was never done, other than to save the reputations of the Kennedy brothers.

I like to think of this book as second generation research into Monroe's death. First generation consideration consists of all the primary sources, biographies, documentaries, commentary and public domain resources. That research has brought us full circle. In the days immediately following Monroe's death the main question was whether her overdose was accidental or deliberate. Today, after many of the conspiracy and murder theories have been debunked, we are again left with same question, was it an accident or was it suicide? I take a different view. I think several other alternatives are possible, and it's these alternatives that will be explored in this book. But for that you will have to wait until Part II of this book. So what is in Part I?

What follows this introduction is Part I, and it's a stand alone story I previously published under the name *Marilyn Monroe: Last Love*. It's a historical narrative that introduces many of the concepts that I've been referring to as the seven keys to unlocking the mystery of Marilyn Monroe's death. Like all historical narratives it mixes actual history and real life characters with elements of informed conjecture and speculation. I want to assure you this speculation is based on facts and sound reasoning. I want to be clear before you read *Last Love* of what my intentions were in writing it. I had hoped it would spark debate. I wanted to nudge people to re-examine the facts in a new and different way. I wanted to invite, maybe even incite discussion. I knew the major premise of the story would be controversial but I had hoped to further explain it by a presentation of posts on an accompanying website. I knew this presentation of the facts would be so large and voluminous that it would never fit into one book. Instead of telling people my theories of what happened, I wanted to bring people to the same realization I discovered by consideration of new and different ways to approach the case.

Last Love ends with a suicide scenario. If you apply Occam's razor to the mass of evidence now assembled, the almost inescapable conclusion would be that Marilyn Monroe deliberately ended her own life. *Last Love* explores one possible reason for Marilyn's suicide. It's actually just a twist on one of the oldest theories available. Regardless of how unlikely it seems on the surface, it's actually a viable alternative to generally accepted "facts." I'll explain why in Part II. Suicide, accident or conspiracy are the three generally accepted answers to the question of Marilyn's death. In the second half of the book, I"ll provide a new "accident" theory. Her death is not a mistake on her part, in this scenario the accident would be in the form of an unintended homicide. The book will close with a murder scenario. In this theory, Marilyn's murder is not the work of a conspiracy, it's the act of one, lone, cold-blooded killer.

There's a popular pseudo-science theory in our current culture that's usually called something like left and right brain thinking. It's generally accepted the right brain is more emotional and intuitive, while the left is more analytical and logical. If you were to apply that concept to this book then Part I will be a result of right brain thinking and Part II would represent left brain thinking. Part I is actually a result of information gleaned in deep mediation. After years of research the information kind of came to me when I stopped trying to think about it. I actually believe the spirit of Marilyn Monroe yearns for the truth to be known and has guided me towards certain truths. If you want to consider it my imagination, that's okay, I'll use logic to back up every important detail disclosed in *Last Love*.

Part II is an analysis of the facts. The left/right brain theory is supplemented by actual science that says both sides of the brain inform each other. This book also represents that view because both parts of the book utilize intuition and logic to formulate possible scenarios that explain not only the facts, but the behavior of the people involved in the moments and years following Marilyn's death. Intuition led me to the conclusion that Marilyn Monroe's death was a suicide, logic won't let me accept that conclusion. It just doesn't fit the evidence as I now see it. So I will present three different scenarios, suicide, accident and murder, and let you decide. By the end of this book you should be armed with enough information to allow you to disregard two of the scenarios. What you are left with may finally answer the question, "Who killed Marilyn Monroe?"

A careful analysis of the Marilyn Monroe case presents an amazing amount of incongruities where nothing really adds up and important conclusions often disagree with each other. A researcher, after sifting through voluminous evidence, is often left with a paradox where two mutually exclusive concepts both appear to be true. Allow me to explain by examples. Most rational biographers come to the conclusion that conspiracy theorists can't be trusted, so all their evidence is suspect. This allows them to dismiss ALL the evidence against any conclusion other than accidental overdose or suicide. Once left with these two options it becomes obvious that it can't be both, it has to be one or the other. But when you pick one, either one, you are left with a paradox. Let's say you think it was accidental. You will find an incredible amount of support for your findings. This was the conclusion of nearly all the people who were close to Marilyn at the time. Her housekeeper, her shrink, her publicist, and many friends on both coasts, all felt it had to be a tragic accident. It had almost happened many times before. But the science says "no." The coroner in the case had always maintained that Marilyn didn't die from taking pills, forgetting she took them, then taking more. Modern forensic science bears him out. Monroe ingested a large number of pills in a short period of time. The amount of drugs that killed Marilyn has been vastly overestimated, but even with the lower estimates that recent science puts forth, a minimum of 17 to 29 pills, that's still too many to take by accident. Plus, she had received a prescription of Nembutal just the day before, with the instructions to take one a day. Wouldn't emptying the 25 pill container have been a wake up call? Wouldn't she realize she had taken a whole bottle of pills in just over 24 hours? It just doesn't seem like it could have been an accident.

So you are left with the other option, suicide. Again you're left with a set of facts totally in opposition to each other. You're confronted with a mountain of evidence from Marilyn's closest companions that say she was not suicidal. There was no note. In a telephone conversation she had just minutes before she would have consumed the deadly dose, she was happy and showed no sign that within the next hour she would decide to kill herself. Things were looking up. Her studio had changed hands and a new contract awaited to be signed. She had plans and meetings for the next week. Several new movie projects were in the works. Other offers for employment were coming in. She was working with an author on a new biography. Suicide just doesn't fit. So what are you left with? It wasn't an accident, it wasn't suicide and it wasn't a conspiracy. Great. The whole case is a mass of contradictions. Here are two more statements that can't both be true. She was having an affair with Robert Kennedy; and, she barely knew RFK. Strong arguments have been made for both. Perhaps the ultimate contradiction in the Monroe case is that Robert Kennedy was in Los Angeles on the day Marilyn died; AND, on that same day he never left a ranch in northern California. On one hand you have the mayor of LA, a couple of police chiefs and multiple eye witnesses that say he was in LA. On the other hand, you have the owner of the ranch, his son, and an employee say RFK was at the ranch that day. Official government documents that detail RFK's schedule seem to bear that out. In my opinion, it's the evidence you don't have that's the deciding factor for this contradiction. Robert Kennedy was at the ranch that weekend with his wife and four of his oldest children. It's more than curious that in over a half a century of Bobby being blamed for murder, never once has his wife or children come forward and stated for the record that he was with them all day on August 4, 1962. Sometimes Kennedy silence speaks volumes.

Lack of evidence can be an important clue in the evaluation of Monroe's case. There are four areas (the first four of the seven keys) that were consistently and effectively denied, downplayed or ignored in the first decade following Marilyn's death. We will see as this book progresses the handiwork of one of the world's greatest spin doctors in making this so. It wouldn't be until 1973, with the publication of Norman Mailer's *Marilyn* biography, that most of the American public would be first introduced to just how close Marilyn was to the Kennedy family. Up until then it was largely kept under wraps. In the years following Monroe's death the lesbian angle of Marilyn's life was only accepted, and discussed by fringe elements with conspiracy theories. It took decades for information about the Cal-Neva weekend to surface. And finally, right up to our present time, no Marilyn biographer has ever investigated the connection of Marilyn's last months to the government's case against MCA. It's these four ignored elements of Marilyn's life that are crucial to understanding what played out in Marilyn's last week. It's these first four of the seven keys that we will examine in *Last Love*, the short story that follows.

Chapter 1

FADE IN:

OPENING SCENE

INT. Frank Sinatra's Apartment.

Marilyn Monroe and Patricia Kennedy Lawford stand near Frank in his living room. Peter Lawford is seated. Pat urges Frank to play his new hit song. Frank pretends not to want to, but is persuaded by the ladies. He strolls over to the record player and puts on, "Come Fly With Me."

Music fills the room. Both women gaze at Frank with starry eyes. Marilyn feels light headed, as if she is breathing rarefied air. She puts her arm around her new friend. She smiles at her and playfully bumps her hips a few times. Then in unison, the two women glide back and forth to the rhythm. Just after a line about being together and hearing angels, Frank lifts the needle mid-song to suggest they all toast to "new friends." Marilyn looks at Peter and adds "and old." She then points at Pat's visibly pregnant belly and sends Peter to the kitchen for juice.

Not wanting a break in the merriment, Marilyn and Pat urge Frank to play more. "Come on Frankie-boy, play some more." "More." "More."

Frank has already walked over to the bar to mix some drinks. But he is not one to disappoint the ladies. "Music there shall be," he says. A magical, sexual energy fills the room. Frank can conjure up charm with the ease of an accomplished and powerful warlock casting a familiar spell. The women aren't sure how he does it, but with the wink of an eye and a devilish grin, Frankie-boy surprises and delights the girls as "Witchcraft" begins to play.

Chapter 2

ANGEL AND HER DEMONS

Marilyn Monroe still has secrets to reveal.

Marilyn loved to keep secrets. They were little parts of herself, she kept just for herself and the chosen few she decided to tell. Her press agent and friend, Patricia Newcomb, was one of Marilyn's closet confidants in the last year of her life. She would remark after MM's death that there was no one that Marilyn told everything to. Marilyn Monroe had a fantastic ability to compartmentalize her life. Susan Strasberg, (friend and daughter of Marilyn's beloved coach, guru, Svengali and father-figure, Lee Strasberg) explained that Marilyn had secret friends, and often one group of friends didn't know about the other unless they met in public.

Marilyn was bi-coastal. Marilyn had homes in both New York and Los Angeles, but in her last year she was "living" in California while only occasionally "visiting" her NY apartment. This was a reversal of how she lived from the late fifties, (the last years of her marriage to Arthur Miller) until about mid 1961.

In those years she knew and befriended a lot of people on the east coast. But in her last year she was much closer to a small number of friends on the west coast. The discrepancy in the reports from these two camps present a problem. It's very difficult to form a complete and accurate reconstruction of Marilyn's last months. We have a wealth of information from her New York friends but are confronted with a near complete wall of silence from her confidants on the left coast.

We have so much information from the Rostens, the Strasbergs, the Greenes, a housekeeper, and from Miller himself, that it's easy to paint a picture of a troubled women, hell bent on self-destruction and destined to take her own life. I want to tell you a different story. The New York-centric view of Marilyn is bleak because it gives testimony to a bleak part of her life. Those years were dominated by disillusion and disappointment. She suffered the loss of two babies and helplessly watched the dissolution of a marriage that she had pegged all her personal hopes and dreams on. Professionally, her career was in a shambles. Her agents and the men she let run her production company were not up to the task and she still wasn't getting offers for the roles she wanted. Her health deteriorated. She was susceptible to sinus infections. The endometriosis and the painful periods she had suffered all her adult life seemed to get worse. She sometimes found it impossible to sleep and would often awake during the night in terror. Tormented by vivid nightmares, Marilyn would identify with the artist Goya and use his graphic portrayals of war and violence to capture the horrific nature of her dreams. She would use an encyclopedia of witches and demons to point out and identify her tormentors. Heart-pounding, pulse-racing, she would suddenly awake with sweat on her brow. For a terrifying moment she would feel caught between two realities, the next moment, certain that she had just escaped death. Lying in bed after one of these nightmares seemed to be like being on the edge of an abyss, or worse, lying in the mouth of a beast who is just waiting to consume you. She would need to get out of bed and find a comfortable chair to curl up in, until the terror subsided. She became hopelessly depressed. And to get through the long, painful, unfulfilled days and the seemingly endless, tortured nights, she became more and more dependent on drugs. Drugs freely prescribed and provided by the studio doctors and the psychiatrists she also came to depend on.

But through it all she persevered. For all her seeming weakness, she was actually quite strong. There was honor in her struggle. She was always able to mount a come back. That is until...

Chapter 3

FRIENDS AND LOVERS

In 1962, the final summer of her life, Marilyn and her publicist Patricia Newcomb were in the middle of a massive media blitz. Marilyn had just been fired by 20th Century Fox and her old studio was waging a very nasty negative campaign against her. Marilyn was fighting back. It's been said that during one of the photo shoots of that time, when Marilyn was feeling tired and uninspired, Newcomb suggested she think of her two lovers to cheer her up.

Who do you think those lovers were? I think the answer will surprise you.

Spoiler alert. One of those lovers is a Kennedy. Okay, that doesn't come as much of a surprise given a half century of pop culture pseudohistory where rumors, lies, mistakes, misrepresentations, misinterpretations, and innuendo have been paraded as facts. But it may not be the Kennedy you think it is.

Most Marilyn Monroe fans have downplayed the Kennedy connection in MM's life ever since the conspiracy theories developed that implicate the

Kennedys in Marilyn's death. Given the results of modern scholarship, and an abundance of evidence, most fans and even some competent historians today concede at least one sexual encounter between Marilyn Monroe and John F. Kennedy. Others see a "continuing" or "episodic" affair between the two. So I will be in the minority when I tell you that for this scenario, there was never even one coupling of this iconic couple. If you are a Marilyn Monroe fan, or have read anything about her death, or participated in the pop culture of the last half of the 20th century; than I may know what you're thinking. You're probably thinking there was at least one. There HAD to have been something going on between them, right? History puts them in the same place at the same time on more than one occasion. And they were after all, Marilyn Monroe and Jack Kennedy, two names almost synonymous with sex. If you have heard any of the tawdry details then you may ask: What about Palm Springs at Bing Crosby's house? Didn't Marilyn's friend and masseur verify that encounter? Wasn't there an eye witness? If not Palm Springs then surely the Presidents birthday gala. What about FiFi Fell's New York party? Or the Lawford mansion in Santa Monica? Doesn't the FBI have records of "sex parties" in the Carlyle hotel in New York? Again here, isn't there an eyewitness that saw MM entering the Carlyle? That's a lot of questions and some interesting possibilities but the answers are simple. Yes to the masseur who did verify Marilyn was with JFK at Crosby's, maybe to the eye witnesses who saw Marilyn enter the Carlyle while a Kennedy family member was also staying there (big deal, she was probably visiting her friend Pat), but a big no to the sex with John F. Kennedy. Those answers may be simple but the explanation is not. By the end of this tale all will be explained and you'll know more about Marilyn's connection to the Kennedy family than if you were to read every book about Marilyn ever published.

If you're thinking ahead you may be saying if not Jack it must be Bobby. But that's jumping too far ahead in the story. First I have to convince you its not JFK and then we can examine RFK's and Marilyn's connection. It *was* her relationship with Bobby that was perhaps the most important relationship in her life, at least it was on the day she died.

But first, back to Jack. There are two friends of Marilyn's that explain the movie stars relationship with the president. It's these friendships that explain why the orbits of these two luminaries would continue to cross paths, and explain why Marilyn was repeatedly in close proximity to JFK. The two dear friends of Marilyn's are Frank Sinatra and JFK's sister, Pat Kennedy Lawford.

Chapter 4

MODERN ROMANCE

The story begins in 1958, a year that would prove
pivotal for Marilyn as well as the cast of characters so
influential in her final months. It's summer and
Marilyn has just returned to Hollywood after a long
absence. The last time she was in LA was two years
earlier, when she was finishing up work on *Bus Stop*.
She had made a movie after *Bus Stop* but it had
filmed in England. Now she was arriving in early July
to prep for the film *Some Like It Hot*, which was set
to begin production in early August. When the press
reception couldn't get past how chubby she was, she
went to repeated efforts to convince them and herself
that the curves were still "in the right places." Of
course even her detractors had to agree that she was
as beautiful as ever. She met the press, then made her
appearance at premieres and other studio required
events with a smile and all the glitz and glamour of
Hollywood royalty. But it was tough.

Marilyn was coming out of an almost year long funk.
In early 1957, after a very rocky start to their

marriage, Marilyn and Arthur Miller were starting to jell. Late spring and early summer would be the happiest time of her life. Marilyn was pregnant and the Millers were renting a cottage in Amagansett. On August 1, while working in the garden, Marilyn doubled over in pain. Later she would lose the baby. In a very real way, and in more ways than the obvious, something in Marilyn died that day and she was never the same afterward. But it wasn't for lack of effort. Arthur Miller would marvel at his wife's spirit and the nobility of her struggle to overcome the adversities that life dealt her.

Unfortunately, the marriage would never be the same either. In an effort to prove how much she still meant to him, and to support her desire to become a serious actress, Miller would adapt one of his short stories into a screenplay. The movie, *The Misfits*, would star his wife in a role that was not in the short story. It would require a whole new concept and Miller would squirrel away for hours, days on end, writing. Months passed. Money was not flowing in. Eventually, they shared a living space but not a life.

Leaving Marilyn alone was probably the worst thing for her. Plus, when Miller would show her drafts he was working on, she was greatly disappointed. She didn't like the character he was writing for her. She felt it was based too much on her and she didn't appreciate the insight it gave her on how Miller perceived her. Miller was a playwright, he was inexperienced writing screenplays and it aggravated Marilyn that he refused to consider her suggestions on ways to liven up the script. There was also a devastating event that occurred about this time that has never been reported. Perhaps it happened at his ex-wife's house when Arthur was on a visit with his children. The exact who and when may not really matter. The important thing to note is, especially when speaking of Marilyn's later infidelities, that in their personal correspondence, it's always Arthur asking forgiveness for a betrayal against Marilyn. Enough said about that. Perhaps the saddest thing for Marilyn was that now Arthur didn't seem to want to even consider trying to have a baby let alone make a move in that direction. Depressed and lonely, feeling dejected as a women and a nonworking actress, Marilyn would turn to barbiturates to get through those previously mentioned endless days and tormented nights.

She needed to go back to work. So here we are, July 1958, and Marilyn is in Hollywood while Miller remained back east, awaiting word from the government on whether he'd be facing jail time for his refusal to name names in the Commie witch hunts. Marilyn greeted her adoring fans and handled the overbearing press. But being the happy, smiling carefree "girl" that everyone still expected was exhausting and she needed a break. She needed a place to get away, but where she could still be around people she knew and trusted. At that time, and in that place, the person she trusted most was Frank Sinatra. Frank's place had been a hideaway before. She was romantically involved with Sinatra when she briefly used one of his hidden hideaways as a refuge after her marriage to Joe DiMaggio. Now at this time, and ever since her marriage to Miller, they were just platonic friends. But Marilyn was sure Frank wouldn't mind her hiding out at his place, and he didn't.

Marilyn requested that Frank bring around some other old friends to get reacquainted. Marilyn had always like Judy Garland and she knew Frank and her were still close. When Frank mentioned Peter Lawford, Marilyn was pleased to meet up with him again. Marilyn liked Peter. She had always thought he was fun and respectful, and she liked his quirky, irreverent sense of humor. And, she was eager to meet his wife, whom she had heard so much about. Their wedding was covered in the press as if they were royalty. Lawford, of course, was married to JFK's sister, Patricia Kennedy.

Marilyn begged off a Gary Cooper party that summer but Frank went, and so did the Lawfords. (It's been erroneously reported that Frank and Peter reunited at this party after a long feud. They had actually buried the hatchet about a month before at the Cal-Neva lodge.) After the party, Peter and Pat stopped by Frank's place to meet Marilyn. Marilyn and Pat hit it off right from the start. Pat was pregnant at the time and the two women bonded over babies. The baby Pat was having and the baby Marilyn still hoped to have. Pat was also excited about her brother John's political future, who as Pat clued Marilyn in, "everyone in the family calls Jack." When she asked if Marilyn had ever meet Jack, Marilyn told her, "Yes, but only briefly." She explained that she had attended an April In Paris Ball the previous year in New York with her husband Arthur and they had been briefly introduced to Mr. and Mrs. John Kennedy.

In 1958, JFK was a senator running for reelection, but Pat, like all her brothers, sisters and parents, was already in campaign mode for the 1960 election. She tried to talk about her brother but dropped the subject after Marilyn seemed more interested in Jackie then Jack. That first meeting was short. They listened to some music, had a quick toast to new friends, and just as the fun was starting it was over. Frank and Peter seemed eager drop Pat at home and go out for the rest of the night.

So there you have the sum total of Marilyn's contact with the Kennedy family through the 1950's. Every other supposed meeting with JFK in the fifties is pure fantasy. The 60's however is a different story. By the time of her death in 1962, Marilyn had met and befriended so many Kennedys, that for a time she was considered a friend of the family.

Marilyn's friendship with Pat Kennedy really picked up steam when the two would meet again in April of 1960. Marilyn had finished *SLIH* near the end of 1958 and shortly thereafter lost another baby. As terrible as losing the first baby was, this time it was even more devastating. Marilyn didn't work throughout the entire year of 1959. Night terrors and the inability to sleep lead her to use more and more barbiturates. She summoned the courage to finally do another movie at the beginning of 1960, but by April it still wasn't completed. It looked to everyone involved that it was going to be a dud. In order to drum up interest in what promised to be a bad movie, the Fox publicity department came up with a plan to create some sexual buzz around the movie by having the two stars hit the Hollywood party circuit together, without their spouses. The "affair" was a publicity stunt, which through a strange set of circumstances became real. In a vulnerable moment Marilyn and her co-star did share a brief, tender time together. With her life and her marriage in taters, he lead her to believe that he cared enough about her to want a future together. Apparently though, he didn't. The movie was called, *Lets Make Love, Then Crush My Heart and Publicly Humiliate Me.* I believe the title was shortened for theatrical release.

Marilyn met Pat again that spring. Pat Kennedy Lawford, the "Hollywood Kennedy" was in full campaign mode. The Hollywood party circuit was just one part of a campaign circuit where Pat rubbed elbows not only with the rich and famous but with political heavy hitters as well. Marilyn and Pat became fast friends that spring. Truth be told, Pat was a little more than starstruck. When Pat was a kid, actress Gloria Swanson had visited the Kennedy home with her daughter. Being about the same age, Pat took the girl around to meet her friends, truthfully introducing her as the famous actress's daughter. Nobody believed her. That wasn't going to happen again and Pat took great pride in introducing Marilyn to her friends. The two began to spend more time together with Marilyn showing Pat how to dress up in disguise to go out in public undetected. Several months later Pat would use this trick to visit Marilyn in the hospital. Enough about Pat for now. I promised you the scoop on JFK, so let's take a look at some Marilyn and Jack stories.

Chapter 5

MARILYN AND JACK

By July 1960, Marilyn had finished that atrocious movie and had returned to New York with Arthur. Marilyn's studio Fox, was demanding she return to Los Angeles to finish last minute dubbing on the movie. The Democratic National Convention was held in LA that month and the week of the convention saw Marilyn traveling across the country several times. Unfortunately in mid-week when JFK decided to make an impromptu speech, Marilyn was not there when he brought her friend Pat onto the stage. When Pat told her she would miss history if she wasn't there for Jack's final speech, Marilyn made it to the convention in time to hear the details of the "New Frontier." It is sometimes insinuated that she "snuck" into LA to carry on her affair with the president. Actually, her low key visit was because she had made an issue with her studio about returning to do work she felt could be done in NY. She just didn't want it broadcast to her studio that she was in town. After the convention, Pat invited her to the Lawfords party to celebrate Jack's nomination.

Marilyn and Frank Sinatra would often go to great lengths to avoid the publicity of being seen in public together. In the past it had been primarily to keep the depth their relationship from Joe DiMaggio and Frank's wife Ava Gardner. Now they had a special friendship they kept private from almost everyone. Sinatra would often arrange for an escort to bring Marilyn to events he would be at. On this night Marilyn arrived at the Lawfords on the arm of Sammy Davis Jr, Frank's friend and fellow Rat Packer. It appears everyone had a grand time as this is reported to have been some party. Contrary to rumor, Marilyn and JFK were not intimate that evening, nor did they skinny dip in the pool. That's patently ridiculous. Did the party get wild? Well it was no Garden of Allah, but near the end of the evening, did a few female guests get thrown in the pool? Did they take off their clothes and briefly frolic naked in the water? If so, it's not exactly scandalous, especially by Hollywood standards. But Marilyn and JFK? No. Marilyn was really just getting to know the future president and she was there as a guest of her friend Pat. Finally, this may be one night JFK wasn't chasing skirts as he was busy basking in congratulatory adulation and couldn't free himself from the hundreds of glad-handers looking for face time with the man who had a good chance at being the next president.

Marilyn wouldn't see Jack again for over a year. Let's take a fast-forward approach to that time and just look at the major moments in each of their lives. JFK was busy for the next several months on the campaign trail. After the convention, Marilyn would fly to the Nevada desert to film her literary husband's debut screenplay, *The Misfits*. Filming this movie made Marilyn miserable. By November, the film was done as was her marriage. Adding to her despair, her childhood idol and fellow co-star, Clark Gable died that month. Marilyn felt deeply guilty that she may have contributed to his death by having him wait so often during the filming of *The Misfits*. That he left a widow who was pregnant made things infinitely worse.

Meanwhile, JFK had won the election. Frank Sinatra had played an integral part in the campaign ever since early in 1960, when JFK made a few stops at "The Summit," the Rat Pack, renamed Jack Pack, bacchanalia party/filming of *Ocean's 11* in Las Vegas. Frank had even recorded the campaign's theme song and was now tapped by Joe Kennedy to produce the inaugural gala.

On the day of the inauguration, Marilyn would fly to Mexico to finalize her divorce from Miller. Shortly thereafter she was so despondent and potentially suicidal that her psychiatrist thought it best to have her committed for her own protection. To show how unlikely a romance with JFK is at this time, contrast Marilyn's life with that of a newly elected president busy with his first 100 days. A time period that would culminate with a national and political disaster in Cuba. After the Bay of Pigs fiasco both the president and his attorney general brother had their hands full, and it wasn't with Marilyn.

Meanwhile, Marilyn was busy thanking ex-husband Joe DiMaggio for extracting her from confinement and finding a place she could recuperate in peace. The two would spend a lot of time together that spring in Florida as Marilyn would work up the courage to finally tell Joe about Frank.

While she was in the hospital, Frank had come to visit Marilyn. They stayed in touch often, with Frank even gifting her a small dog for companionship. He also made it clear that she was welcome to move into his place anytime she wanted. There had always been obstacles to a romance in the past but now they decided to give it a go. She moved into his home. Frank traveled a lot, and could never be faithful to just one women for long periods of time, so Marilyn did eventually get her own apartment in LA. She also kept her NY place. It was hard to pin Frank down, but their time together in the spring and summer of 1961 went well enough for Marilyn to hope that a marriage proposal would soon be coming. Sooner or later Frank would want to settle down. Marilyn planned to make it sooner.

The next time Marilyn would see JFK was when she was traveling with Frank and they were very much a couple. In early fall, Peter Lawford was filming the movie *Advise and Consent* in Washington, DC. Frank was invited to appear in a cameo. Frank invited Marilyn along. If you've ever heard the story where Marilyn traveled up and down the Potomac in a motorboat with JFK, Hubert Humphrey and a few of their aides, it's true and happened during this visit in the fall of 1961.

While in DC, JFK let Sinatra know that because of all the hard work that Frank had done on the gala, Joe Kennedy was inviting Frank to his house for a special dinner in his honor. Earlier in the summer Papa Joe had extended an invitation to Frank to join the Lawfords when they visited him and his wife in the Riviera. That invitation had been rescinded and this was a way to smooth things over with Frank.

During the fall of 1961, Rose Kennedy, Joe's wife and Pat's mother, had decided to stay in Europe and visit Paris while Joe returned to Hyannis Port. JFK wanted his father to have a good time and knew Frank would bring the party to the compound. Aboard JFK's private plane, a disguised Marilyn joined the Lawfords, Frank, the rest of his entourage, a dozen bottles of champagne, cases of wine and other party fixings and flew to a small airport near Hyannis Port. Marilyn got to personally gift Joe Kennedy the Italian bread that Frank brought. JFK's wife Jackie got angry at the goings on and this weekend would prove to be the beginning of the end of Frank's cozy relationship with the Kennedy clan.

Many people will deny that Marilyn had anything to do with these events and offer bogus proof she was elsewhere. (All they really prove is the lengths Marilyn would go to avoid revealing information about her outings with Frank, to DiMaggio.) It doesn't matter. The point of the story is there was nothing sexual going on with Marilyn and JFK. Marilyn and Frank are definitely a couple at this time, plus she is traveling with her friend Pat. The next time she would cross paths with the president occurred shortly thereafter and it would be as a guest of Pat in her Santa Monica beach home.

The moments JFK had spent with Marilyn in DC, and then at his parents house, sparked an intense interest in him for Marilyn. He soon began to look for ways to meet up again with her, preferably with neither Frank nor Jackie around. The president would take a trip that fall to Santa Monica and attend an informal dinner given by his sister in her and Peter's beach home. Marilyn would be in attendance that evening. (This is the same JFK visit where he is "spotted with Marilyn" during a formal fundraiser "at a Beverly Hills hotel." Often in the retelling, the formal, and very public, fundraising part is left out.) The informal event at the Lawford home is important because it will become the genesis of every JFK/Marilyn affair story in the future. Bits and pieces of what happened that night will themselves fragment and show up in a variety of stories set in different times and places. To permanently cement this meeting in the lore of every conspiracy theory is the fact that Marilyn and the president's escapades that evening were taped.

By the fall of 1961, everyone from J. Edgar Hoover to Jimmy Hoffa had heard of the wild goings on at the Lawford beach house, more commonly known as the

"Western White House." Whoever was eavesdropping on that particular day hit the jackpot when the president hustled Marilyn into an empty room that happened to have a live bug. With no time to spare, because someone could come into the room at anytime, Jack tried to make every second of alone time with Marilyn count. As for JFK's moves... he was direct, quick moving, up close and extremely personal. He slipped his arm around her waist and pulled her so close that he seemed beside her and in front of her at the same time. She felt a whirl of hands all over her body until one hand rested on the small of her back. As they locked eyes inches apart he never stopped talking. In that charming accent, his words were so smooth and creamy they seemed to drip with anticipation.

Marilyn, surprised yet flattered by the attention, at first could only get out his name as a question. Jack? Jaack? Finally in mock protest, she said in a way only she could, a very breathy, "Mr. President." It was all the encouragement he needed as he slipped the hand on her lower back under the elastic waistband of her capris. He cupped her behind and told her she had the nicest ass in Hollywood. With pouted face and that Marilynesque mixture of sensuality and vulnerability she whispered, "Just Hollywood?" As they laughed he leaned in even closer and kissed her neck as his hand went even lower. He firmly pressed against her and leaned in so close his face was almost in her bosom. She was sure if he leaned any further they would both topple onto the floor. Just then fate intervened and it was suddenly over. Pat knocked on the door, then slowly opened it looking for Jack. JFK laughed and told his sister he was just getting to know Miss Monroe a little better. Pat muttered a quiet, "Uh huh" as she escorted Marilyn out of the room.

In the retelling of this encounter, the tale usually morphs into a dinner party with Marilyn seated next to JFK. In some reports it occurred at Puccini's during the week of the convention. It usually goes something like this: JFK's wandering hand travels up Marilyn's thigh, when suddenly, the president realizes she isn't wearing panties as his fingers enter the promised land. Afterward, Marilyn tells some reporter or close friend that she found the president "very democratic" and/or "very penetrating." Sometimes one of those lines is used but in a different context, with Marilyn describing a totally different kind of sexual encounter with JFK. Like all Monroe/Kennedy stories they get a little crazier with each retelling.

Later, back in reality, the audio recording of this night would be spliced together with an actual sex tape of JFK (most likely with his mistress Judith Campbell Exner) to make it seem as if things progressed way further than they actually had. This recording would prove to be a huge aggravation for Joe DiMaggio, and would end up costing someone a large amount of money for it to disappear. Because many people heard the tape before it disappeared, their first hand evidence would be used as proof of a JFK/Marilyn affair. But that one encounter, more of a flirtation than anything else, would actually be the extent of the "sex" John Kennedy had with Marilyn Monroe. After that evening JFK would attempt to spend a night with Marilyn but would never consummate his plans. Well, probably never. They would meet only three more, well documented times.

The next meeting would be at social event in New York, a party at socialite Fifi Fells Manhattan home in February 1962. Some reports mistakenly have this party a few months later. Another confuses this party with a different Fell/JFK party the previous year. Peter Lawford's business partner, Milt Ebbins was there with Marilyn, so his account is the most reliable. Before the party Marilyn assured Pat nothing would happen. Did she keep her word?

Before we arrive at the Fell party lets take a moment to reminisce. Let's go back to the night JFK ushers Marilyn into a quiet, empty room. When Pat had asked Marilyn what had happened that evening in her home, Marilyn had told her it was just Jack flirting. When asked what she did, Marilyn exclaimed, "I flirted back." She assured her friend it meant nothing. But other guests that evening knew of Marilyn's alone time with the president and it caused a bit of concern as the rumors spread. Marilyn convinced Pat the whole thing was just silly. But when Marilyn added with a grin, "unless he really means it," Pat grew concerned all over again. She knew what that meant.

Back in September, around the time of the party in Hyannis Port, both Marilyn and Pat thought Frank was on the verge of popping the question. He had given Marilyn an expensive set of earrings that both women thought was a prelude to a ring. It hadn't happened, although Marilyn was still hopeful. Pat knew that if Marilyn thought Jack would someday marry her, she would be terribly disappointed, so she warned her about how her brother could be with woman. Marilyn assured her she knew exactly how to handle Jack.

If Marilyn were looking to start a new sexual adventure this would be the time. Marilyn was having man troubles. Miller was gone, Frank was absent, and DiMaggio was... well... complicated. Arthur Miller, her ex-husband of just one year had moved on. When Marilyn came back to New York in early February 1962, she learned Miller was soon to be married to a photographer he had met while filming their movie,

The Misfits. The fact that the woman was already pregnant was like adding salt to an open wound.

Meanwhile, Frank seemed to be pulling away. Sinatra was a busy man. He traveled around a lot. He appeared regularly in Vegas and in late fall of the previous year he went on a world tour through Asia. He was often reported in the press to be romantically involved with someone new. And of course Marilyn heard the rumors of other women, but she had a special bond with Sinatra, and still thought marriage was possible. But as 1961 was about to end, she found her self alone. Pat was with the Kennedy family back east and Frank was nowhere to be found.

During Christmas of 1961, Joe DiMaggio made a repeat appearance in Marilyn's life, as he had the Christmas before. He knew how depressed Marilyn could get around the holidays and didn't want her to be alone. Joe and Marilyn had a unique relationship. He could be good for Marilyn, especially during rough times. He was like a buoy she could hold on to during the times she felt most like drowning. His friendship and companionship meant a lot to Marilyn but both of them knew they could never be married to each other again. A relationship like theirs just didn't work. He would never be okay with her career, and she could never be okay without it.

When Marilyn met JFK at the Fell dinner party in New York she may have felt like she was single. She had heard the rumors about Frank and Juliet Prowse throughout the previous year, but in January 1962, the press was reporting the two were to be married. It came as a complete surprise to Marilyn and she did not take the news well. She really felt that if anyone was to be the future and final Mrs. Sinatra, it would be her. She confronted Sinatra with how hurtful it was finding out this way but he downplayed the whole thing as a publicity stunt. He said he was "just helping the kid out." Marilyn wanted to believe him but she had a fabulous B.S. detector and she just wasn't sure.

One thing she knew about Sinatra was that he would never apologize, especially about another woman, but he would try to make it up to her. In this case that would turn out to be a trip to Mexico he arranged for

Marilyn where she could shop for furniture for her new home on his dime.

For some time now, Sinatra and Monroe had been talking about future film projects they could do together. During her stay in Mexico, Sinatra was going to arrange for Marilyn to meet Albert Maltz, a screenwriter he wanted her to consider. Back in early 1960, during the time Sinatra was involved in JFK's campaign, he had hired Maltz to write a screenplay. It caused quite a stir. Maltz was a victim of early Hollywood blacklisting because of communist ties and he lived in Mexico in a small community of artists branded by the U.S. as "Commies." John Kennedy had been alright with Sinatra's business dealings with Maltz as long as Frank held off on the announcement until after a crucial primary. But it was not alright with Kennedy's father. Papa Joe had given Sinatra an ultimatum, "It's Maltz or us." But that was during the election. Frank thought now it might not be an issue. When Sinatra told Marilyn that Maltz lived in a community that included Frederick Vanderbilt Field, America's exiled silver spoon communist, he told her she might want to run it by the president just to make sure he would be okay with it.

So that was one thing on Marilyn's mind when she met JFK at the Fifi Fell party. Another was a discussion she had with the presidents brother Bobby, just the week before. So while Marilyn did have a few things to discuss with the president, she wasn't naive. She knew that Jack was interested in more than talk. Peter Lawford, JFK's brother-in-law/Hollywood connection, had for some months now been telling Marilyn how special the president though she was. Even indicating that he might want to spend the night with her. Marilyn was intrigued and wondered just how special he thought she was. But she had also told Pat that nothing would happen. She decided to meet Kennedy that night and make it clear that she wasn't interested in being a conquest. She was playing for keeps now and if something were to happen, she wanted that something to have a future.

There are reporters who swear that JFK and Marilyn snuck out of the party, then used secret tunnels to rendezvous in Kennedy's room. Who can say for sure. Marilyn assured Pat nothing happened and perhaps, we too, should take her at her word. After this dinner party Marilyn would meet up with JFK two more times.

The next meeting would be when Marilyn and JFK were both guests at Bing Crosby's home near Palm Springs at the end of March, and the last would be the night she sang Happy Birthday to the president in May.

Chapter 6

MARILYN AND BOBBY

Up to now we haven't mentioned Robert F. Kennedy very much. It's time to insert RFK into Marilyn's story. Bobby wasn't present at Hyannis Port when Marilyn was there. By the time they were introduced Marilyn had already met most of the family. In addition to Pat and JFK, Marilyn already knew Joseph Kennedy and had met Kennedy sisters, Eunice and Jean as well. It was after Hyannis Port that Pat told Marilyn that the sibling she really wanted Marilyn to meet was her brother Bobby.

Pat and Bobby were close. Close in age and ideals. Pat, Bobby, Jean and Teddy were the youngest of the nine Kennedy children and they descended in age in that order. Pat deeply admired Bobby. He was a crusader. He was thoughtful, considerate, compassionate and the most religious of her brothers. But he was also tough. It was said that being the runt of the family made him feel he had something to prove. He was a determined fighter and competitor. Pat admired not only his desire and bravery, but also his capacity to make difficult decisions and his determination not to compromise on what he felt was right. RFK's detractors thought he was ruthless, someone even once called him a "narrow minded moralist that would use any means to get to his ends."

In the mid-fifties RFK was selected as chief council to Senator McClellan's Rackets Committee that was investigating the infiltration of organized crime into labor unions. It was then that Bobby picked a fight with the mob, that would turn into a crusade, that would dominate his time and attention while he was attorney general. By September of 1959, Bobby had resigned from the McClellan committee and decided to write a book about his experiences there. He felt the committee's 300 plus days of hearing testimony from over 1500 witnesses had uncovered significant corruption in labor. He also felt that most of the unions were cooperating and voluntarily ridding themselves of racketeering. It was only the Teamsters, headed by Jimmy Hoffa that refused to clean up their act. And it was Hoffa and the Teamsters that would play staring roles in the book RFK was writing.

RFK's book was titled *The Enemy Within*. After it was published, Papa Joe would pull some of his Hollywood strings to get the book turned into a movie. As it turned out, it was Marilyn's studio, 20th Century Fox, that would decide to make it. This brings us to Robert Kennedy's initial interest in Marilyn Monroe and their first meeting.

There are two dinner parties given by the Lawfords at their beach home, both with MM and RFK in attendance, that are often confused and conflated by Marilyn biographers. Most have a dinner in February, 1962 as the time they first met, but they actually had met many months earlier in the fall of 1961. It occurred in the period between the events at Hyannis Port and the time Jack got handsy with Marilyn. Pat was eager to introduce Marilyn to Bobby and Marilyn was intrigued when Pat said that Bobby wanted to meet her.

On this occurrence Marilyn was driven to the Lawford home by friend/make-up man Whitey Snyder. You may have heard the story where Marilyn pulls up, exits Whitey's VW bug, then tells the surrounding press that the driver was a sailor she'd been seeing. Knowing she would be surrounded by young, beautiful Hollywood starlets, she decided to dress to impress and put on the sexiest little number she could find. She was actually a little embarrassed by her choice and got tipsy drinking when she learned that Bobby only wanted to talk business with her. It turned out that his wife Ethel was impressed with Marilyn's acting abilities. She thought that Marilyn was under-appreciated, and she wanted her to play Ethel's part in the movie, *The Enemy Within*. Bobby also wanted to gather information about MCA, the talent agency that represented Marilyn.

If you've ever heard the story where RFK and his press aide Ed Guthman drive Marilyn home after she drank too much, then deposit her in her Doheny Drive apartment, this is that night. Marilyn hadn't yet bought her Fifth Helena Drive home, which she would be in the process of buying when she would meet RFK (this time with Ethel) at the Lawford home in the beginning of February 1962. This dinner party is usually presented as their first meeting and the story usually goes something like this: Marilyn has heard Bobby is interested in meeting and talking to her. She isn't sure what to talk about so she goes around to various people and solicits questions on current topics she can ask the attorney general. She writes these questions on cards, on a clipboard, or in a notebook, or sometimes even on napkins in lipstick!

Believe it or not, the stories have some factual truth but it's actually all a rouse. It's an awkward attempt by Marilyn to be clandestine. She did have the notes and made quite the public display to have people overhear her questions. But once in private, (they went out for a walk and ended up talking in a parked car) Marilyn had answers for Bobby instead of questions. You see, the previous fall he asked Marilyn to get information concerning MCA, the talent agency that represented her in Hollywood. Marilyn was relaying her latest information.

The MM, RFK and MCA story is so complicated and so integral to Marilyn's final days that it will be looked at in more detail in Part II of this book. For now let me fill you in on some of the backstory. When

RFK became attorney general he began an almost single minded pursuit to finally nail Jimmy Hoffa, a prize that as of yet had alluded him. He organized his Justice Department for this pursuit in a way that Hoffa described as a "vendetta." It's hard to argue with that observation as Bobby's main priority was overseeing his "Get Hoffa" squad. But he also had other areas in the Justice Department under his control that he was less interested in, and less knowledgeable about. One of those areas was the Antitrust Division.

Just weeks after RFK took the AG job, he was notified by the head of the Antitrust Division that MCA was being investigated and if the evidenced warranted, it could lead to a grand jury with civil and criminal charges being brought against them. MCA was a Hollywood power house that not only represented the top stars but produced movies and TV shows as well. Since MCA controlled the production of the majority of the TV shows that aired in prime time the FCC wanted to investigate as well. The FBI had been conducting it's own investigation since 1959. Many of Hollywood's power elite that helped JFK become president had ties to the top men at MCA, Jules Stein and Lew Wasserman. The problem for the Kennedy brothers was that both men had ties to mobsters as well. In 1961 the term "organized crime" was a fairly new concept and most Americans had yet to hear of the Cosa Nostra. But when Robert Kennedy became Attorney General his top priority became ferreting out the top criminals and sending them to prison. This probably explains RFK's pursuit of MCA. It wasn't just their aggressive business practices that got Kennedy's attention, it was also their suspected connections to underworld criminal activities.

Stein had started in Chicago during Prohibition booking bands into nightclubs controlled by Al Capone. Wasserman got his start in Cleveland working for gangster Moe Dalitz and his gang, promoting their nightclub, the Mayfair Casino. Wasserman married the daughter of an attorney for Dalitz. When Dalitz moved his operation to Vegas and became the owner of the Desert Inn, the

Wasserman's were frequent guests. Both Stein and Wasserman did business with Jimmy Hoffa, and both relied on the services of "fixer" Sidney Korshak in sticky labor relations negotiations. Connie Bruck, author of "*When Hollywood had a King,*" thinks Korshak was perhaps Lew Wasserman's closest friend, and notes that Wasserman never disavowed the friendship, and Mr and Mrs Sidney Korshak celebrated their fiftieth wedding anniversary at the Wasserman's' house. Korshak was known as the "Mouthpiece for the mob in Hollywood." According to the organized crime division of the Justice Department he was "the brains behind the mob." To retired FBI agent William Roemer, "He was the primary link between big business and organized crime."

After the Bay of Pigs fiasco, RFK would increasingly try to get information from sources outside the government. RFK's aides called the individuals that he got information from "meta diplomats," what we might today call confidential informants. Marilyn Monroe isn't usually portrayed as a bright, astute, business minded woman but she was all these and more. Marilyn had switched to MCA when she formed Marilyn Monroe Productions with Milton Greene in the mid-fifties, and had been working with them ever since. She provided Bobby with valuable inside information and background that other witnesses were reluctant to give. Throughout the first months of 1962, this passing of information about the MCA case, along with talking about RFK's movie, would be the reasons for all their time together (a couple walks on the beach at the Lawford home) and all the phone calls to Washington. Their relationship was purely professional, at least through the spring of 1962. The president's birthday event at Madison Square Garden would change things considerably.

When we left our discussion of JFK to segue into RFK we were left with two final prospects for a MM/JFK romantic connection, Crosby's in March, and the birthday event in May 1962. With the Madison Square Garden event we can kill two birds with one stone, because neither JFK or RFK had sex with Marilyn Monroe that evening. So lets take a look at that night and save Bing Crosby's for last.

We'll look closely at what's been called the Palm Springs tryst soon. But now we're going to consider the aftermath of that eventful weekend. After Marilyn and JFK were both guests at Crosby's home rumors started to fly. Government officials in Washington were especially scandalized when Marilyn's name showed up on a list of entertainers for the president's birthday celebration. However by that time, at least for Marilyn and Jack, whatever the MM/JFK flirtation was, it was over. Marilyn had even called the president shortly after the weekend to say, "Hey, no hard feelings, right?" The two did now share an unspoken bond and there was never, ever, any animosity between them. Nor was there any more romance.

Marilyn had committed to performing at the birthday event and nothing was going to stop her from being there for the president. JFK was fine with her performing, but it seems he was the only one. There was some political pressure to have her removed that proved unsuccessful. And on Marilyn's end, the studio that once agreed to let her go now was refusing it. That didn't work out well for them, because Marilyn went. Of course it didn't work out great for Marilyn either, because once she was in New York, she was served breach of contract papers from FOX. Bobby had assured Marilyn, that because of Kennedy family connections on the board of the studio, that she would be okay in coming. He had let her down and she was already a little angry when he showed up in her dressing room before the show. She had no idea that Bobby himself didn't want her there.

Bobby was a man on a mission. What had been a friendly, professional relationship between the two suddenly turned uncomfortably personal. The two had their first heated exchange that day. Their only argument worse than this one would occur on the last day of her life. Bobby was intent on having Marilyn tone down her performance because word had gotten out that it was getting progressively sexier each time she practiced it. She was offended by not only what he was saying, but how he was saying it. It felt almost like bullying. Marilyn asked, "Exactly what do you think I'm going to do." She then began gyrating and whipping her head back and forth in a mock strip tease. This just angered RFK. Before he left he declared that "The kiss" on the cheek after the gala as JFK comes onstage "is out, you can't do it." With that he opened the door, stormed out, and muttered something to a smirking bystander as he slammed the door behind him.

Marilyn decided to do the kiss anyway. Originally she wasn't scheduled to be the last performer. It was a last minute change to liven up the finale and also to provide the running gag where Marilyn is introduced over and over, then finally appears at the end. When she was finished singing, JFK would take the stage and she would greet him with a birthday peck on the cheek. It never happened. Both Marilyn and JFK expected it. If you look at the footage of that evening really close, as Kennedy comes on stage you can see Marilyn behind him being escorted down an aisle offstage. JFK even looks back a few times to see where she has gone. This little change in the program would reveal Bobby's objective for the rest of the evening, keep Marilyn away from the president.

At the after party, Robert Kennedy is said to have fluttered around Marilyn like a moth to a flame. And indeed he did. He was running interference. He took it upon himself to personally keep JFK and MM apart that evening. Pat Kennedy Lawford's job (she knew better and was just playing along) was JFK, she would keep him distracted and busy elsewhere. RFK even recruited Marilyn's press agent, friend, and companion Patricia Newcomb, so if Marilyn got past him, she would intercept MM. It was all very silly. Marilyn knew exactly what was going on and even had a little fun making Booby (her name for RFK who was, apparently, a big fan of cleavage) dance around her all evening. It would also prove to be not the only time Newcomb and RFK would conspire together for a common goal in regards to Marilyn.

Not exactly the beginnings of a great romance is it? And it never would be. There was never an intimate encounter between MM and RFK. Confused?

Did I hedge my bets when I said there was never a MM/JFK sexual encounter? Well, if there ever was one, and it didn't happen after the Fell party, then it probably happened in Palm Desert, the home of Bing Crosby near Palm Springs. And it's this weekend where we shall now turn our attention.

Chapter 7

A TWIST ON THE PALM SPRINGS TRYST

It was JFK's sister Pat who was instrumental in getting Marilyn to Crosby's that weekend. Originally the plan was for the Lawfords and Marilyn to meet JFK at Frank Sinatra's home. At Bobby's insistence, because of Frank's mob ties, (Sam Giancana had stayed at his home) the location was changed at the last minute. Frank was furious and took off to Bermuda to blow off steam. Marilyn feared Frank begrudged her continued closeness to the Kennedy family while he was on the outs. Maybe he secretly harbored resentment that she was the reason he was being pushed away. At any rate, Marilyn wasn't sure she wanted to attend. In New York, just about six weeks earlier (the Fell party), she had let Jack know that she was playing for keeps now. There would be no conquest, no sneaking around, and any "relationship" had to have a future. JFK had backed off and both knew nothing was ever likely to happen.

But Pat knew that her husband Peter had oversold his pathetic pitch for MM to "spend some time alone with the Prez." He had built up the idea in Marilyn's mind that JFK was more interested in her than he obviously was. Pat knew Marilyn may never believe how Jack was with women unless she saw him in action. After JFK's last discussion with Marilyn, and with the way Frank was behaving, JFK never expected Marilyn would attend. So he invited a couple of White House secretaries on the trip. The famed duo known to history as Fiddle and Faddle came with JFK to Palm Springs.

Pat idolized her older brother but she had to dispel these notions Marilyn had of a possible future with Jack. She knew her brother and knew the secretaries would be there. She persuaded Marilyn to meet her at Crosby's and arranged for Peter to get her there. Peter, nor anyone else, would ever tell Sinatra that it was Lawford and Frank's friend/partner Jimmy Van Heusen that would arrange for the location to be changed to the secure and very private Crosby home. When Marilyn arrived the president was surprised. He wondered if this was a positive sign. Then, sensing an opportunity, JFK sent the secretaries to the press parties at the surrounding hotels.

Marilyn, the Lawfords, JFK and a few other guests enjoyed an afternoon by the pool. After dinner inside, Jack invited Marilyn back to his quarters. Marilyn glanced at Pat looking for signs of approval. Pat just shrugged as if to say, "It's up to you." Curiosity got the best of Marilyn as she retired to the president's private room. Once in the room Marilyn saw Jack grimace in pain as he sat down. Determined to make the president's back feel better, she offered a massage.

Marilyn's expertise in anatomy took many forms, but one of them was a near therapists knowledge of muscles, movement and massage. She impressed the president but still had to verify what she was talking about with a call to her masseur. After the call things were progressing. Jack said that for him to be truly comfortable they should go back out to the pool.

Giggling, hand in hand they rushed out to the pool. Jack dispatched his Secret Service detail and had them watch the large yard from another building on the property. Fortunately the pool area was empty.

Inside the home, the drapes had been drawn along all the windows, so no one could see from inside the main house. It had been a warm day but now the temperature had started to cool. Marilyn dipped a toe into the pool to see if the water was still warm, then she slipped off her robe. The presidents back must indeed have felt better because when Marilyn looked at him, he too was already naked. The presidential flag proudly waved over the compound at full staff. After a shared smile and brief moment of mutual appreciation, they jumped into the water together. Marilyn wrapped her arms around the president's neck and rested them on his shoulders, then said, "I'm so glad you changed your mind." Jack realized immediately there had been a misunderstanding and he tried to jokingly let her know that this may be a one time thing. When she asked about what to expect in the future, he broke her heart with a joke that she wasn't "first lady material."

The Secret Service had the home locked down and the agents on the outer perimeter were just following normal procedure when they let the returning Fiddle and Faddle into the compound. Just when Marilyn thought the situation in the pool couldn't get much worse, the secretaries (or Twittle and Twattle as Marilyn called them) bound onto the patio like new born deer, and with fake surprise exclaimed, "What's going on here?" As they giggled, Marilyn got out of the pool, wrapped her robe around her shoulders, clenched it in front, and with as much dignity as she could muster, walked past them and said, "He's all yours girls." Once in the house and fearing a complete collapse she quickly moved to Pat's room and knocked on the door.

Marilyn knew Pat would be there for her, she always was. And she knew Pat would be alone. Peter and Pat didn't share a bedroom at home and rarely spent the evening together when traveling. Peter was undoubtedly at the press parties, or wherever the action was, and wouldn't return until morning. Pat opened the door and almost immediately Marilyn broke down in her arms. Pat held her as she cried, feeling guilty for her part in whatever just happened. She had never thought it would go so far. Marilyn kept sobbing, "I'm such a fool. I should have listened to you."

Pat and Marilyn were very close friends. They enjoyed a unique and special relationship. One evening about a year and half earlier, it was fall of 1960 around the time of the election and also just before Arthur Miller walked out, the Lawfords and Frank Sinatra visited Marilyn in New York to cheer her up. They had all just returned from Hawaii and they heard Marilyn was having a tough time. Just like the evening Marilyn first met Pat in 1958, Peter was eager to leave. Like last time he left, but this time Frank stayed and the remaining three shared a lovely evening together. It was a crisp autumn night with a beautiful moon and a crystal clear sky. It was a great night to view the city lights from the air. Frank's plane was on standby and he persuaded the woman to take a midnight flight on what he called *El Dago*. Sinatra knew the ladies would enjoy the view.

Something surprisingly intense happened that night. Marilyn developed deep romantic feelings for Pat, but she never even imagined that anything could ever happen between them, even though she was sure that Pat felt the same way.

This night was shortly after filming *The Misfits*, and we've seen the troubles Marilyn had a few months later and how her personal problems were tearing her apart. So much so, that in early 1961 she was eventually hospitalized. There was a long stretch of many months that Marilyn didn't see Pat. In June of 1961, Marilyn would reunite with the Lawfords when they all met Frank in Vegas for Dean Martin's birthday. Pat was pregnant with her fourth child and wasn't sure how to tell Marilyn because she knew how badly Marilyn wanted a baby of her own. When Marilyn first met Pat she was pregnant and seeing her now brought up that fond memory. She was overjoyed and jumped with excitement when she saw that Pat was pregnant. She put her hands on Pat's belly. Pat told her it seemed like the baby jumped with joy as well. Pat was so slim that Marilyn couldn't believe how far along she was, and with her hands still on Pat's belly, said, "Oh my, she must be no bigger than a robin's egg."

Pat asked Marilyn to be baby Robin's godmother but Marilyn declined, fearing her presence would cause a media frenzy that would take attention away from the special day. Pat had met Marilyn after a Gary Cooper party, so Cooper's wife and Pat's friend Rocky, seemed like a good sentimental second choice. Marilyn and Pat grew closer and closer. They talked so often on the phone they began to share confidences that they told no one else. In person they would exchange even more intimate secrets. Marilyn would tell Pat of her past encounters with women and Pat always seemed interested in learning more. Marilyn told her of an affair with Natasha, her old drama coach. She told Pat that Natasha was too much like a man. She acted like a husband, always barking orders and giving directions. But there was one thing Natasha did well. In Natasha's own words, she "held the cure" for what Marilyn needed when she was tense and needed to relax. MM and Pat shared a laugh when Marilyn exclaimed, that "Unfortunately the same mouth that held the cure also had to tell the world about it!"

There was always a sexual undercurrent to Pat and Marilyn's relationship. But nothing ever really happened. Society stigmatized same sex relationships with scorn, ridicule and contempt. It was the early sixties, homosexuality was still considered a mental illness, Pat was Catholic and a Kennedy, AND the presidents sister, and she was CATHOLIC. But still there was something there. Stolen glances, flirting smiles, lingering touches and warm embraces. But there was a line and it was never crossed, until...

In a Crosby bedroom, Pat held Marilyn until she realized Marilyn was wet and she was shivering. Pat got a towel. She slipped the damp robe off Marilyn's shoulders and let it drop to the floor. Marilyn shivered now for a different reason as Pat rubbed the towel over her nude body. Pat took Marilyn by the hand, led her to the bed and had her sit on the edge. Marilyn sat naked in front of her as Pat helped Marilyn dry her hair. Marilyn wept, continuing to say, "I'm such a fool." Pat sat next to her friend on the bed and held her until she stopped crying. Once again Marilyn softly said, "I'm such a fool" but this time added, "Who could ever love me?" Pat put her hand on Marilyn's face and gently turned her head. Then lightly resting her forehead on Marilyn's, she looked her in the eyes and said, "I have always loved you and I will always love you." With that Pat rises and again stands in front of Marilyn. She begins to unbutton her blouse. Moist lips part, then come together. No more words are necessary.

Human scissors cut the bonds of thousands of years of sexual repression. In the morning, the two women awoke entwined in a loving embrace. It was then that Pat uttered a mere four words that contained a sentiment Marilyn had waited a lifetime to hear. Pat smiled and whispered to Marilyn, "You're a Kennedy now."

Marilyn was elated. She finally belonged. She loved and was loved back. She was wanted, appreciated, and valued. Marilyn knew they could never have an open, public, love affair. Was this night a one time thing? A shared intimacy that could never be repeated? It didn't matter as long as Pat was in her life. She had finally formed a deep and meaningful bond with another human being, and it meant the world her.

Chapter 8

THE KENNEDY AFFAIR: A NEW WRINKLE

The next time she saw Pat, Marilyn was a little nervous. Marilyn decided on a surprise visit to Pat's home where she found her on the beach with friends. Marilyn dressed in orange and black, sported cat-eye glasses, and carried a bag with a small stuffed animal tiger to give Pat as a gift. Marilyn was sure Pat would get the inside joke. She dressed in honor of Frank, because he had in more ways than one, brought them together. Orange and black were favorites of Frank's and Sinatra loved to dress in those colors. Ever since the three of them had spent the night together, Marilyn and Pat shared a secret pet name for Frankie. When the two were alone together they would call him Tiger. They would giggle about how the phrase "Put a tiger in your tank" took on a whole new meaning.

Pat was surprised to see Marilyn, so things got awkward quickly. Neither was sure how to act in front of other people, so Marilyn made up the excuse that she was there for the president's phone number. It was a partial truth because Marilyn did want to smooth things over with Jack after the Crosby weekend. JFK had left early Sunday morning, so the last she saw of him was when she left the pool. About two months after their "swim," and just days after the birthday gala, Marilyn would decide to have a little fun teasing the president about what he had missed out on at Crosby's. She posed nude, in and out of the pool, on the set of the movie she was filming, *Somethings Got To Give*. She would make sure the photos made the covers of magazines on newsstands around the world. No one could miss it, not even the president. That it knocked Liz Taylor off the covers was just an added bonus.

With Jack squarely in her rear view mirror, the view forward was foggy. How to proceed would be a problem that would vex both women, right until the moment Marilyn died, which would now be only a few months away. At first both agreed to tell no one about what had happened. It seemed the best for everyone. Marilyn especially needed time to come to terms with it and she was the first to break their pact by telling her psychiatrist. At least she told him in her own way. Knowing Dr. Greenson would disapprove she had to talk around it. She told him her feelings for women were starting to surface, asked how to cope with it, things like that. She told him how tremendous the fear was that she would be exposed and how the information becoming public might ruin her career. She was vague and not at all specific in what she initially told Greenson. But then she finally confided to Greenson that she had followed through on her feelings. She never said a word about Pat to the doctor. Instead she told him about a situation she put herself in with another young actress, one that hadn't worked out well.

Then one day Marilyn, while having lunch with Pat, let the cat out of the bag about telling Greenson. She wanted to explain that she never told her doctor any details, but she couldn't because they were at a lunch date that included a last minute addition of one of Pat's friends. Pat got defensive because she feared Marilyn had disclosed too much to Greenson. Upset, crying and unable to explain, Marilyn got up and made a hasty exit, hoping that Pat wasn't angry with her.

Pat wasn't as angry as she was concerned. It had to be difficult for her too. She had told Marilyn that she was closer to her sisters Eunice and Jean than to anyone else in the world, and she didn't think she could even tell them what had happened at Crosby's. If you want to gauge how the family would have reacted in 1962 think about how things still are today in 2017. Are there any Kennedy's today that live an openly gay lifestyle without fear of being cut off by the family? You would think that with the dozens of nieces and nephews of Ethel Kennedy and Jean Kennedy Smith there might be at least one.

Peter probably knew, without ever having been told. His and Pat's marriage had basically been for show now for many years. All Pat demanded was a modicum of discretion. Peter was aware, and apparently alright with Marilyn spending more and more evenings with Pat at the Lawford home. When the oldest Lawford child began to notice how affectionate his mother was with Marilyn, he was told that she was "like a little sister" to Mommy.

Jack was the only person in the Kennedy family Pat could confide in. She knew she could trust him. He was the only one in the family that wouldn't judge her harshly. Many years earlier, when Pat's older sister Kick had fallen in love with a married man, ten years older and, heaven forbid, a Protestant, Jack was the first in the family she told. He supported his sister when the man divorced and the two decided to marry. Shortly after, Kick tragically died. It was Jack (and Kick's example) that gave Pat the resolve to marry Peter, a man also outside the Catholic faith, who agreed to raise their children in the church. Jack was supportive then. But could Jack accept this? He did, but he also counseled what she already knew. It could never become public knowledge and keeping what had happened under wraps would be difficult but it would be of the utmost importance. With a wink he tried to lighten the situation and added, "At least until after the next election."

Pat didn't want anyone else, especially Bobby to know. At least not at first, probably never. Pat knew that for Bobby, Eunice and her mother, it would be a toss up as to whether a lesbian affair would be more detrimental to the family name or to Pat's immortal soul. Papa Joe could never be told. Marilyn had heard the rumors about Pat's sister Rosemary, so she knew that Pat's parents could never find out.

Marilyn felt that Bobby would be key to any future she hoped to have with Pat. After their argument in New York, Marilyn was determined to have Bobby "like" her. Even after all that Frank had done during the election, she saw how Bobby just cut him off cold. It was brutal and she didn't want the same thing to happen to her. After she was fired from 20th Century Fox, she sought his help and advice. She also wanted to discuss the strange way the MCA case was playing out. Marilyn was worried about backlash from the Screen Actors Guild and from fellow actors if her role in the case ever became public. She had every reason to be worried. The men who ran MCA were heavily connected, not only in the southern California political scene, but also by the mob connected lawyers they hired. There was more going on behind the scenes than anyone has ever realized.

By the end of 1961 both Kennedy brothers became aware of the bugs that had been in the Lawford home. They went to great lengths to make the "Western White House" safe and warn all family members to be careful in conversations and NEVER assume any phone conversation to be secure. Because of the added scrutiny the eavesdroppers had to find alternative methods of getting new information.

By the end of June of 1962 the rumors about Marilyn and JFK had subsided, but new ones concerning Bobby were beginning to spread. The MCA case would provide kindling for these rumors and by the end of July these smoldering embers had turned into a raging wildfire. Decades after the fact when people began to "remember" an affair between MM and RFK, what they are actually remembering are these rumors.

It's claimed Marilyn herself is responsible for some of these rumors and that may be true for a couple of reasons. First, she was still in contact with Bobby for reasons already stated; her firing, the MCA case, and now also the trouble RFK was facing getting his movie made. She still felt she had to be "clandestine" in her conversations with Bobby, so she sometimes characterized those meetings as a "date." Second, I'd like you to consider that something else might be going on here. Marilyn wanted to be playful, plus, at times she could wear her heart on her sleeve. She lived from a place where only feelings are real, so she may have wanted at times to share a piece of herself with those around her. She loved Pat and wanted the world to know, but that was impossible. She wanted to be part of the family, yet knew it had to remain secret. So I'm suggesting that, what is happening here, is a playful yet secret way of disclosing the truth. Something along the lines of: Marilyn teases, "I'm seeing a Kennedy!" Stunned bystander says, "The President?" Marilyn winks and says, "No, the other one." It's the assumptions that the other one is Bobby is what's being repeated.

So in the summer of '62, all of Hollywood had heard the rumors of Marilyn and Bobby, including many who wanted to use that information to get Bobby off their backs. Somebody in that large group of people, put a wire on Marilyn's phone. They were quickly disappointed about an affair but at the same time they were presented with an opportunity. They lucked out when RFK made plans to visit Marilyn's home. In an effort to get on Bobby's good side, and show how stable and independent she was, Marilyn invited him to see the home she had bought that year and was in the process of fixing up and decorating. With no affair to work with, and in an effort to make something from nothing, a plan was hatched by our nefarious eavesdroppers and evildoers. A photo of Marilyn and Bobby at her home might prove useful. They had no idea how lucky they would get.

Marilyn had a small house but it had a pool, patio and a large backyard. Beyond the pool and patio the yard stretched backward ending in a group of trees and a fence shared by the neighbors backyards. It was remote enough that with access from the neighbors yard it made a great vantage point from which to photograph the back of Marilyn's house. Conveniently given the date and time of his arrival from a phone call Marilyn made to Washington to confirm Bobby's visit, a photographer was in place when RFK, driven by the Lawfords, arrived at Marilyn's home. The Lawfords stayed in the house while Marilyn gave Bobby a tour. As fate would have it she led him out to the patio hand in hand.

Was a photo taken? Was the photo used as leverage to get Bobby to back off from his relentless pursuit of the criminal underworld? If that was the plan it completely backfired. Bobby dug in his heels and decided to fight back. He had enough trouble keeping his brothers real affairs secret, he wasn't going to back off because of a fake one. He doubled down on his efforts to expose the evil he felt was overtaking America. The script for his movie was nearing completion and the search for actors had begun. And as for MCA, the case took a monumental turn.

RFK had a bulldog named Leonard Posner as the chief investigator in the MCA case. Like many in the

Justice Department he wanted to see MCA prosecuted for violating the Sherman Antitrust Act. In mid July 1962, RFK decided to unleash the hound. On July 13, RFK sent a shock wave through LA by charging MCA with violating antitrust laws. The government placed a restraining order on MCA and wouldn't allow it to sell off it's talent agency. Plus they threatened to block MCA's takeover of Decca Records which owned Universal Studios.

It was feared criminal charges against MCA and the Screen Actors Guild would have been disastrous for Hollywood. Many in Hollywood decided to back MCA and denounce the government's actions. There was a widespread fear that TV and movie production would move elsewhere. Marilyn feared she would become essentially "blacklisted," or worse, if her participation in the case became public. Suddenly the rumors about her and Bobby weren't funny anymore. People were starting to assume Bobby was doing this for Marilyn because of the split she had with MCA. She wanted answers and Bobby was backing away and ducking her calls. She heard that Sidney Korshak (reported mob lawyer with connections to the Chicago syndicate and MCA) was involved. She set up a meeting with Korshak to find out what was going on.

Frank had returned from an oversees tour in June, and Marilyn now turned to him for advice and protection. When Frank had found out about the Marilyn and Pat weekend at Crosby's he left the country. At least that's how it seemed to Marilyn. For a guy who supposedly didn't like to travel he sure went on a lot of world tours. This time he'd been gone from April well into June. Back in February, her publicist's idea to get Frank jealous by suggesting Marilyn date an ex-bullfighter in Mexico had been a dismal failure. (Maybe by design because her publicist didn't want Marilyn with Frank.) Frank did not come running as he had with Ava eight years earlier, when she starting seeing a bullfighter in Spain.

Neither Pat Lawford nor Marilyn had seen much of Frank for many months but when he did get back it turned out that he was more supportive than anyone. He was genuinely fond of Pat and the feeling was reciprocated. He knew how close the two had become.

He was, after all, there that evening in late 1960 when the three of them spent the evening together and took the midnight flight over New York. Marilyn called that evening her "fling on a wing." Something she had never tried before.

Pat and Marilyn provided the lift for the flight as they coaxed Frankie's fuselage to fly skyward. Then the women settled in to enjoy the view and the ride. Flight Frankie was mostly about him that night but everyone did reach their destination, happy and content. It never happened again, but Frank had definitely noticed how the two touched and looked at each other, and how their relationship would cool immediately afterward, (maybe because of shock, surprise, confusion or concern) then really deepen a few months later.

Frank was happy when Marilyn finally told him, although he doubted Pat would ever tell anyone about what happened. He knew it couldn't ever become anything serious, but he saw how happy she was and couldn't burst her bubble. He even joked he was okay with being Marilyn's beard, and then in all seriousness, asked her to marry him. He knew that no one would ever mess with her if she was Mrs. Frank Sinatra. They wouldn't dare say a word. Marilyn seriously considered his offer. It had actually been one of the plans Pat and Marilyn had considered. That night at Crosby's they talked of how Pat would stay married to Peter. Marilyn would marry a willing partner to the arrangement, then they could live in close enough proximity to maintain the relationship. Marilyn dreamed of other plans as well.

Marilyn knew of Pat's ambitions when she came out of college. Pat wanted to be a producer. She had come to Hollywood with that intent but soon encountered the glass wall. It was a male dominated profession. Marilyn thought she could change that by having Pat run Marilyn Monroe Productions, with Pat not only producing, but some day directing Marilyn's movies as well. She was already making concrete steps in that direction with Frank Sinatra and with the Lawford owned production company Chrislaw. Marilyn was talking with Frank about many projects. One was going to be an *Ocean's 11* type caper on a train.

Marilyn was planning a future that she was eager to get to. Frank was happy to help. Frank even offered his Cal-Neva lodge for her and Pat to get away to. He promised that no one would ever bother them there and contrary to some rumors about rooms in the lodge, the cabin would not have cameras or listening devices. It turned out it was a promise he couldn't keep. A photo was taken at Cal-Neva that would change the lives of nearly everyone mentioned in this story so far.

Chapter 9

PHOTO FINISH

The Cal-Neva resort has a long and storied past that reaches all the way back to the days of prohibition. It was actually built with secret tunnels to facilitate bootlegging. At least that's the legend. Others say that Frank Sinatra built the tunnels after he bought and renovated the place (with gangster Sam Giancana's money) in the early 60s. The lodge was built by a wealthy businessman in the 20s to entertain friends. It's situated on the north shore of Lake Tahoe, one of the most beautiful lakes in the world. Lake Tahoe straddles the border of California and Nevada. It's in the Sierra Nevada Mountains, fairly close to Reno. The state line that dissects the lake goes right through the resort. The Nevada side of the Cal-Neva is home to one of Nevada's oldest casinos. It got it's gaming license shorty affair gambling became legal in Nevada. Through the years it became the playground of not only the rich and famous, but mobsters as well. It was also a favorite haunt of JFK's father, Joe Kennedy. Old man Kennedy not only liked to visit, he had

Christmas trees sent back east every year. Our interest in the Cal-Neva begins in the mid-fifties when gambler Bert "Wingy" Grober bought the place. There's a famous photo of Marilyn Monroe and Frank Sinatra dining at the Cal-Neva. In the photo a white haired man standing behind the seated pair leans over between the two. That man is Wingy Grober.

Wingy got the money to purchase the place as the result of a "lucky" hot streak at a mob owned casino. Lucky is in quotes because the streak was said to be courtesy of his mob friends as a way of disguising the mobs share in the casino. An ownership percentage that eventually found it's way to Sam Giancana.

You see Wingy Grober was not a lucky man. Like most gamblers Grober would often find himself broke and in need of financial help from some friends. In Wingy's case that usually meant mafioso's. Grober also got into trouble with the IRS. For help with that mess Wingy turned to a friend who just happened to be an expert in paying the least amount of taxes possible. That friend was the greatest manipulator of the U.S. financial system that ever lived, Joseph P.

Kennedy. Joe Kennedy knew how to make money and keep it as well. If "Greed is good," then Kennedy was the Gordon Gecko of the 20s. But Gecko's power pales compared to Kennedys because unlike Joe Kennedy, he was never appointed chairman of the Securities and Exchange Commission. It's said that Papa Joe had made sure each and every one of his kids had a million dollars in their name BEFORE the great depression. And old Joe had a lot of kids. In terms of today's buying power, each child started their adult lives with about $14 million. The Kennedy's were rich. Joe's wife Rose liked to point out that they weren't Rockefeller rich, but Joe surely had a top 20 fortune. At times he would find creative ways to put (hide) that money into secret investments. One of those appears to be an investment in the Cal-Neva. He not only gave Wingy advise on his taxes, he likely paid them as well. So now Kennedy, at least by his reckoning, owned a large share of Wingy's holdings in the hotel and casino.

In the spring of 1958, old Joe made an offer to Frank Sinatra that he couldn't refuse. JFK wouldn't officially enter the race for the presidency for another year and half but his old man was already lining things up for the campaign. Joe Kennedy was going to sell his son Jack like soap-flakes and part of that marketing effort involved wowing the Hollywood crowd. Joe had little faith that his actor/son-in-law, Peter Lawford, could get the job done. Peter's old friend Frank Sinatra was a different story. Frank could not only could bring on board his fellow celebrities, he could pass the hat around to gangster pals as well. The only problem was that Frank and Peter had had a falling out years earlier. Kennedy persuaded Sinatra to mend that friendship, then do what ever it took to get JFK elected. Sinatra and John F. Kennedy were kindred spirits and Frank needed little persuading. But to sweeten the pot, Joe Kennedy promised to sell part of his share of Cal-Neva to Sinatra at a sweetheart price should JFK win the nomination at the Democratic National Convention set to be held in Los Angeles in 1960. That summer in '60, John Kennedy did win the nomination and Frank Sinatra and his pals became owners of the Cal-Neva. Now exactly who owned what, and at what percentage, became a contested matter, and the matter would simmer below the surface until it finally blew up in the summer of 1962.

When Frank took over ownership of Cal-Neva he had big plans. The hotel had a short season, it was only open in the summer. Snowy, mountain roads made in hard to get to in the winter. So to make the place accessible year round he built a helicopter pad. He also built a large new concert hall and new cabins. Frank's big plans came with a big price tag. It was going to take a big loan to make it happen. Enter Sam, aka Momo, aka Mooney, Giancana. Frank and Giancana had probably already been making plans as early as that spring or summer of 1958 when Joe Kennedy first proposed the idea. That summer Giancana was hiding out with Sinatra in a small Indiana town during the shooting of Some Came Running. He was ducking Robert Kennedy and the Rackets Committee.

Some versions of history have Joe Kennedy sitting down with Sam Giancana and making a deal. It's likely it never happened. What is likely is that Joe Kennedy used Frank Sinatra and had him make the deal. Kennedys "deal" had probably been nothing more than a blanket promise to all donors that when elected JFK would remember the people that had helped him get there. How much Sinatra embellished on that deal can't be known. What's almost certain is that Giancana thought there was a deal. But I'm getting a little sidetracked.

Back to the Cal-Neva expansion. Frank turned to his friend and fellow owner, Giancana for the money. In the past, one call to Teamster's president Jimmy Hoffa would have got Momo as much money as he needed. With the pressure RFK was applying to Hoffa, the large loans at sweet rates had disappeared. A smaller loan from a bank was arranged but Giancana himself had to put up his own money for the expansion.

The exact details are a mystery, but by 1962 Momo felt the Kennedy's owed him. Any way he looked at his mental ledgers had him coming up short. Giancana must have felt that Kennedy never owned as much of Cal-Neva as he thought, thus Joe couldn't give Sinatra and his pals such a large share. Now, if old Joe still felt he had points, Momo wanted the Kennedys to put up a share of the money that went into the renovation. This was on top of what he wanted to be paid back for the time and money he "donated" (now money lent with interest due) to JFK's campaign. With Joe Kennedy having a stroke at the end of 1961, Kennedy made his demands for a payback directly to the president. He used JFK girlfriend and mobster honey, Judith Campbell as a courier of messages to the president. JFK had attempted to payoff Giancana, but the money he sent through Campbell wasn't enough.

Momo was testing his strength. He knew he had Bobby in check. By May 1962, the CIA was advising RFK not to prosecute Giancana because they had enlisted his help in assassination attempts on Castro. RFK was also learning just how much the Chicago Outfit had helped with his brother's election, as well as his father's numerous ties to the very men he was investigating.

Giancana wanted money and his crony Johnny Rosselli wanted the IRS off his ass. Giancana, again with messages sent through Campbell, demanded a "summit," a face to face meeting with RFK. The date this historic face off was to occur? The last weekend of July 1962.

This was the reason for Sam Giancana's now famous utterance caught by a bug. A statement never fully understood by biographers and researchers. "I'm going to get my money out and I'm still going to own half the joint." He was going to get the money out that he put up for the renovations AND he was still going to own his rightful half of the place.

To guarantee RFK would show up and not pull a fast one, Giancana let it be known that while Joe Kennedy and his son Jack had visited Cal-Neva, they had been secretly videotaped. Maybe as a sign of good faith, Momo would to turn over his treasure trove of tapes.

RFK had agreed to the meet. What exactly was planned for the weekend we may never know. It was said afterward that it would have been the "big fall" for Bobby. RFK went west and was in LA on the

Friday before the scheduled meet. But something happened that changed history. A tip came in the LA field office of the FBI that an assassination attempt on Bobby's life had been planned. RFK made a hasty exit from LA back to Washington. Bobby couldn't now risk the meet, it could never be kept a secret from the J. Edgar Hoover and the FBI. (It turns out it wasn't kept from Hoover. A few weeks later Hoover sent Bobby a memo about his father and Cal-Neva.)

Someone had to confront Giancana to find out his end game. It was a family matter and Pat Kennedy Lawford demanded that she could go and have Peter hear Momo out. The brothers balked at first, but Pat was strong willed and independent. She was going to go. JFK and RFK reluctantly agreed when Pat pointed out that neither Sinatra nor Giancana would let anything happen at their place. Pat trusted Frank implicitly. She finally persuaded her brothers everything would be okay by telling them she would bring Marilyn along. Sinatra would never allow anything to happen that would have put Marilyn in danger. The meeting was arranged. The Lawfords and

Marilyn arrived in Lake Tahoe to find Sam Giancana already in lobby.

(As a side note to this story it would be Frank Sinatra who would end up paying the debt Giancana felt he was owed. Frank and his pals did it by performing "free" concerts at various times throughout the remainder of 1962 with the proceeds going into Momo's pockets. But on this last weekend in July, tensions were high and nothing had yet been settled.) It's at this this point we now resume the story.

Pat and Marilyn were alone in one of Frank's private cabins when Marilyn got sick. She hadn't been well all day, but none of them were. The day had been draining for everyone. Peter had beaten a path to Frank's door many times since arriving and had just left on another mission, when Marilyn began to vomit. They hadn't left the cabin for hours, so Pat immediately flashed on one of Marilyn's most persistent paranoias and thought "the food was poisoned." All the food had been brought to them that day and Marilyn hadn't hardly touched her dinner. After Frank ate Marilyn's desert, Pat had given Marilyn hers. She had only taken a few bites. Pat thought that if it was poisoned she may have eaten enough to make her deathly ill. Many of the other events of that weekend proved to Pat that maybe Marilyn wasn't wrong to be paranoid. The threat was real. Pat had known that for weeks but now her eyes were opened to just how serious things had become.

The Kennedy sister knew Marilyn was bright and intuitive. Marilyn could get the gist of a book from just reading small parts, and she had an amazing ability to read people and their intent. Plus, she was smart and informed enough to know the gravity of what was going on, even though Pat could not tell her the details and extent. Even Pat didn't know everything herself, and now was just as confused as Marilyn. What she did now know was that Marilyn's fear and paranoia wasn't just caused by the increasing number of pills it took for her to sleep. The pills made it worse but the threat was VERY real.

This night she didn't know if it was drugs or something worse but Marilyn was violently ill. Did Marilyn take something while she wasn't looking? Things were stressful that day and she was medicated, but she seemed fine. The two of were talking when Marilyn's face took on a peculiar pale shade of green. She didn't look well at all. Before Pat could ask her if she was feeling okay, she had bolted towards the bathroom. Pat followed and found her kneeling before the toilet. Marilyn had stopped vomiting and now looked like she was about to pass out. Pat knelt down beside her and tried to hold her up over the toilet. She held her for a moment and then the two thought it was over. Marilyn felt a little better and she rested her head on Pat's shoulder. Suddenly, vomit spewed out again all over both of them. Again Marilyn clutched the bowl and tried to purge into the toilet. But she could only dry heave. This continued until once again she felt that the worst was over. Both women stood. They were a mess. Pat had a hard time getting Marilyn's blouse off. Between Pat trying to hold her up and Marilyn's twisting and turning, her top had become bunched up and was restricting her arms. Once Pat had Marilyn's soiled blouse off, she removed her own. Needing to get Marilyn cleaned up, and with hopes that it would revive her, Pat turned on the shower. She was horrified as she turned back toward Marilyn. Her face was now blank, she had taken on a shade of gray and looked like a ghost. Her eyes rolled up. Her knees began to buckle. Pat was able to grab her before she fell, but she had difficulty holding her upright. In the struggle that followed, Marilyn bending in half, spun around and got drenched from the waist down before falling to the wet floor.

Perched by the toilet, Pat tried to hold on to her but Marilyn kept losing consciousness. This was something completely different from anything Pat had seen Marilyn go through before. A previous weekend at Cal-Neva, when she had fallen out of bed and remained unconscious, it had only taken a splash of water and a lot of coffee to rouse her awake. This weekend she had complained of feeling ill when they arrived but she had rebounded after resting. Now Pat was holding Marilyn in her arms fearful that she was going to die. Marilyn was having trouble breathing. Suddenly her eyes bulged and her tongue looked swollen as she gagged and shuddered. She then passed out.

Frantic, Pat knew she needed help and ran to the phone to ring the switchboard. Nearing hysteria, she ordered the operator to have Peter return and to have Sinatra summon a doctor. A few minutes later, Peter, who was already on route back to the cabin, arrived to find his wife in a state of panic like he had never witnessed before. She grabbed Peter's arm and explained what was happening as she rushed him towards the bathroom. As they approached they heard Marilyn gasp, then start coughing. Peter helped a groggy, but now conscious Marilyn up while Pat wrapped a towel around her shoulders. Marilyn was cold. She was already wet and didn't want to get in the shower. So after drying off a bit, the Lawfords helped her out of the bathroom.

Meanwhile, Sinatra's pal Skinny D'Amato who managed the Cal-Neva, had been notified of the emergency immediately after Pat had called the front desk. He knew there was a doctor in the casino. He dispatched a bellboy to retrieve the doctors bag from his room. He instructed one of his people to notify Sinatra and then he went off into the casino to locate the doctor. He had seen him drinking earlier and now hoped he wasn't plastered.

When Sinatra was notified he was in his private cabin with two guests; the face and acting leader of the Chicago syndicate, Sam Giancana, and Johnny Rosselli, the Outfit's Las Vegas "Strategist." Immediately, Sinatra bolted towards the hidden tunnel that connected the two cabins. Giancana and Rosselli were close behind with Rosselli grabbing Sinatra's camera on the way out.

While Pat helped Marilyn to a chair she instructed Peter to go find Sinatra and a doctor. After sitting for just a moment, Marilyn decided she wanted to lie down. Pat told Peter, "Go, I'll help her over to the bed." Peter was leaving as Frank was arriving and the two stopped long enough for Peter to explain the immediate need of medical attention. Frank told

Peter to go to the casino and help find a doctor. Their pause was long enough for Giancana and Rosselli to rush past. As the gangsters arrived in the room, a startled Marilyn leaned into Pat sending both women to the floor. Giancana raced over to the women to help. Marilyn was on her hands and knees. Pat was already starting to stand when Giancana stood behind Marilyn and awkwardly grabbed her by the waist to help her up. Johnny Rosselli was across the room standing close to the doorway taking pictures!

Sinatra burst into the room and when he saw what Rosselli was doing he knocked the camera out of his hands and screamed, "What the hell are you doing?" The odd trio across the room; a topless Marilyn, Pat wearing a bra, (but because she was standing behind Marilyn looked like she was also nude from the waist up) and a very surprised but seemingly amused Sam Giancana; were momentarily frozen like deer in headlights. With wide eyed wonder the three watched the camera fly across the room and crash against the wall. An angry Rosselli grabbed Sinatra, pointed at the busted camera and exclaimed, "We're gonna take that." An angrier Sinatra grabbed Rosselli by both hands, drew Rosselli's face to own, pushed him toward the wall, and in the most menacing tone he could muster screamed, "Over my dead body!" Rosselli was prepared to make that happen. He already had a hand on his revolver when Sinatra let go, clenched his fist and was about to strike Rosselli. A now very serious Giancana put an end to the scuffle with one word. "FRANK!" Realizing his "dead body" outburst could actually happen made Sinatra freeze in his tracks.

A stern look from Giancana as he shook his head back and forth was all that was needed to tell Rosselli to back down. Another tilt of the head towards the door told him it was time to leave. Peter, who was blocking his way, raised his hands and jumped backward to let him pass. When Peter had went out the front door he had spotted Skinny D'Amato heading down the hill leading another man with a black bag towards the cabin. Peter had come back to assure everyone a doctor was on the way, but now with mouth open, he couldn't get out the words. What seemed like an eternally long, tense, silent, frozen moment was broken when Marilyn began swaying. Peter rushed over and helped Pat get Marilyn into bed. Pat then took charge and yelled at the men to "GET OUT!"

It was a decisive moment for the man sometimes called Mooney, a man so crazed that in his younger days people thought he was a lunatic. First, nobody gave him orders, but he had already decided to leave. His problem was Frank. Frank was his buddy and had been for a long time, but Sinatra had just disrespected one of the Outfit's top men. He couldn't allow Sinatra to push Rosselli around like that. Rosselli was a fixer and had been connected to the Chicago syndicate for decades. He was now in a top position, acting as kind of an ambassador between all the major crime families in Vegas. It was now Giancana who had to find a diplomatic solution to the current problem. He looked at the camera but didn't move towards it. Instead he just left. As he passed by Sinatra he sneered "We'll settle this later." Then the underworld boss followed Rosselli back into the tunnels.

Frank grabbed the camera and told the others that he would find a doctor. As he was leaving, Peter told Frank the doctor was coming, but Frank ignored him. Pat looked at Peter and said, "Get us out of here." The plan had been to leave in the morning but when Peter caught up to Frank he persuaded him to make arrangements for them to leave that night. Frank didn't need much persuasion. He was extremely angry and believed Marilyn had just almost overdosed. He thought Marilyn needed more help than she was getting and wanted her to check into a hospital so she could reduce her growing dependence on drugs. He completely misread the situation and was livid that she could let this happen and also blamed the Lawfords for not stopping it.

Frank told Peter that he would make sure Marilyn was alright and then he wanted them ALL gone. Eager to return to the casino, the doctor briefly attended Marilyn. He wasn't sure exactly what happened, but when he heard about Marilyn's traveling pharmacy, he too, thought it was the drugs. When the doctor relayed Pat's concern to Frank that it may have been the food, Sinatra just scoffed and said that was impossible. Later that evening when Marilyn and the Lawfords were leaving, Sinatra pulled Peter aside, looked him dead in the eye and with a bone-chilling delivery growled, "Never come back."

Chapter 10

THE FLIGHT FROM CAL-NEVA

Safe now. On board Sinatra's private plane. Heading to the airport in San Francisco. In an attempt to calm his frazzled nerves Peter grabs a glass and a bottle of Frank's best booze and heads to the rear of the plane. Pat is a rock. Pat is a champion. Seemingly calm and composed, a terrified woman hiding behind a stoic Kennedy face, holds the person she loves most dear. A physically and emotionally drained Marilyn rests her head on Pat's shoulder and curls up into a tiny little ball. Pat puts her arm around a trembling Marilyn and pulls her close. The interior lights are dimmed and both women stare at the array of tiny lights in the ceiling which resemble a night sky with the stars overhead. In the background, Judy Garland serenades them with the song "Who Cares?" (It had become kind of a theme song for Marilyn and Pat that last summer.) With the way they cared for each other, both women were sure the song was written just for them.

A warm wave of security washes through Marilyn and she finally feels safe. Marilyn begins to muse.

Silent and motionless.

Nothing was spoken.

Everything was felt.

A couple

together.

Together as

one.

Marilyn's hand finds Pat's and their fingers interlace. Each of their bodies moves instinctively for the comfort of the other as they shift and then nestle again into place. Their love spans realities and sustains universes. Peaceful and content, they both close their eyes and begin to slumber. When Pat feels Marilyn's head lower ever so slightly, she knows Marilyn is falling asleep. Pat kisses the top of Marilyn's head and wishes her sweet dreams. Marilyn smiles and drifts away.

Both women sleep as the plane begins its descent. Turbulence awakens Pat with a start. Marilyn continues to slumber, blissfully unaware that her worst nightmare has already begun.

Chapter 11

ALWAYS ON THE TARMAC

FINAL SCENE

A brisk gush of air and Marilyn suddenly awakes.
When she looks around and sees no one, she fears
she's alone. She stands and notices Peter passed out
in a nearby seat, but Pat is nowhere in sight. Puzzled
and woozy she searches her memory and tries to
reconstruct the days events. The door to the plane is
open and once again she feels the breeze of cool night
air coaxing her to clarity. She rushes to the door and
pauses. She sees Pat on the tarmac talking to two men.
She knows instantly that these are not Sinatra's guys.
She has been followed by the FBI enough times to
know two G men when she sees them. Pat must have
reached Bobby. Marilyn flashes back to a
conversation she had with Pat before they left Cal-
Neva. Pat had assured her everything would be
alright. (Both women were almost certain that it was
something Marilyn ate or drank that made her sick,
but Pat continued to deny that it could have been

intentional. Pat tried to hide her fear that it was she herself, and not Marilyn, that had been the target. Nor could she admit to Marilyn the possibility that once Bobby had been warned of an assassination attempt in LA, the plan had changed, and now any Kennedy was game.) All Pat would say is that she had to talk with Bobby. Her brother would know what to do. They had to trust him and do exactly as he said. Marilyn remembered Pat mentioning Hyannis Port so she reasoned that Pat must be heading there to meet Bobby in person. But surely she would say goodbye before she left.

When Marilyn sees Pat and the men stop talking and start to walk away she quickly emerges from the plane and yells, "Pat?" A chill goes up Marilyn's spine as she steps into the cool night. The cold steel steps give her bare feet the sensation of walking on hot coals and she rushes down the stairs and then runs towards Pat. When Pat hears Marilyn call out, she stops and tells her companions to, "Go on ahead, I'll catch up." Pat starts walking to meet Marilyn. The agents walk a few paces forward then stop to wait near their car. Marilyn sees the impatience in their faces but then turns her attention to the approaching Pat.

A sliver of moon hangs in the sky. Serpentine clouds to the south and the bright lights of the airport obscure the twinkling stars of the night. It's cool and breezy. Marilyn wraps her arms around herself and vigorously rubs her upper arms. She flashes a questioning smile as Pat arrives. The night feels more like early fall in Connecticut than summer in California. Pat takes her own jacket off and when she gets to Marilyn she wraps it around her shoulders. With a sheepish look as if to say "I'm sorry," Pat explains that she didn't have the heart to wake Marilyn up. Before Marilyn can object Pat steers her back toward Sinatra's plane and says, "Honey, we have to get you back inside, you'll catch your death out here." Pat was concerned. She knew all to well of Marilyn's nightmarish ordeal with a reoccurring sinus infection that had plagued her all spring. And now, after the days events, she was so weak and sick she needed rest. Marilyn could read the concern on Pat's face. Pat had told Marilyn earlier that she really thought she was going to die in her arms on that bathroom floor at Cal-Neva.

MM: I'm feeling better. Really. I'm going to be okay. Where are you going? What's going on?

PKL: Peter knows what going on. Didn't he tell you anything?

MM: Peter's asleep.

Pat's eyes momentarily dart toward the plane and Marilyn sees a look of disgust and disappointment flash on Pat's face. Pat's relationship with Peter was strained and Marilyn had seen that look all too often. Pat explains she had just spoke with Peter, he must have passed right back out.

PKL: It's bad Marilyn. Very bad. I'm flying home. I have to talk to Jack and Bobby in person... NONE of us can talk by phone. You can't say anything to anyone about what happened. You know that... Don't you?

Marilyn nods, disappointed that Pat called Hyannis Port home. She constantly called her Santa Monica home the "beach house," like she was on an extended vacation. Marilyn tries to hold her words back, but her furrowed brow and worried, inquisitive look betray her desperate desire to ask Pat to take her with. Both women know that is impossible.

One of the agents walks around the car and gets into the drivers seat. The pilot has emerged from behind the plane and is now standing at the steps. The other agent starts to walk toward the women but stops short, not wanting to intrude. Because another plane is taking off nearby he has to yell, "Mrs. Lawford, we really must be going." Pat turns briefly toward the agent and raises a finger signaling it will be just one more minute, then looks back at Marilyn and flashes a reassuring smile.

PKL: Go back with Peter. He will get you home. He'll make sure you're alright. You can even stay at the beach house if you want. You can trust Peter.

MM: Apart from you, I don't know who to trust or what to do.

PKL: We both have to trust Bobby. He will know what to do. We HAVE to do what he says. I will have

Peter come by to fill you in. Until then just do what you would normally do.

The agent yells out, "Mrs Lawford I really must insist..."

This time Pat ignores him and is about to say goodbye when Marilyn interrupts.

MM: Don't say goodbye. Goodbye can be forever.

Marilyn discreetly moves her hand forward to touch Pat's fingers. For a split second Pat recoils as to not divulge their secret. But then Pat grabs both of Marilyn's hands with her own.

PKL: Okay, how about, I'll see you soon.

MM: Promise...

PKL: Promise.

Marilyn mouths the words, "Love me." Pat can't tell if she has said it as a question or a request. It doesn't matter, her reply will be the same. She mouths the word that means so much to them both. "Always."

Every since the night in Palm Desert when Pat told Marilyn that she had always loved her and always would, the word had taken on a special and sometimes even playful meaning for the two women. It perfectly described the deep, multifaceted and eternal feelings they had for each other, all ways and always. They loved each other in every way and forever more.

Marilyn watches Pat turn and walk towards the government car. Sinatra's pilot stands at the stairs to the plane with one hand on the steel railing. Dressed in dark clothes, the bright lights of a luggage carrier behind him give form to a black silhouette, an empty void that makes him appear as if he is part of the night. As Marilyn gets closer his grim face suddenly smiles, and with his other hand out like a maitre d', he say's, "Shall we." Marilyn slowly climbs the steps and once at the top pauses to look back at Pat. One of the agents is holding the door open as Pat gets into the car.

The pilot stands right behind Marilyn and gently puts his hand on her back, smiles and says, "After you, Miss Monroe." Marilyn looks at the pilot, she forces a half smile and nods her head. The bright interior lights of the plane illuminate Marilyn's face. Her eyelids instinctively lower as she steps into the doorway.

Pat is seated in the backseat of the government vehicle. She looks toward the plane hoping to see Marilyn one more time but the agent is obstructing her sight. When he finally moves Pat catches one last glimpse of Marilyn as her shock of blond hair disappears from view.

FADE OUT.

Chapter 12

SUICIDE SCENARIO

Marilyn took the Coke can in her hand and swirled the contents. She knew it couldn't be more than one swift gulp or she wouldn't get it down. She also knew that along with the coke, the can already contained enough chloral hydrate to put her to sleep. She set the can down by the sink in the guest bathroom and looked at her reflection in the mirror. Did a frightened Norma Jeane just watch as a determined Marilyn opened the Nembutal bottle and then slowly, painstakingly pull apart a capsule, empty the contents into the small opening at the top of the can, discard the empty pieces of capsule into the toilet, then repeat the whole process over and over again until the Nembutal bottle was empty?

"Drink it down and you can sleep with your babies tonight."

Marilyn dropped the empty coke can in the wastebasket, flushed the toilet and made sure to take the prescription bottle so housekeeper, unwanted companion, and Dr. Greenson spy, Mrs. Eunice Murray would be none the wiser. Marilyn also grabbed the slip of paper that she had been clutching for the previous few hours and left the bathroom. She noticed the house phone wasn't in the changing room. She had called Dr. Greenson to tell him about her call from Joe's son, then she had taken the phone out to the guest house. A phone jack had been installed in the guest house so the house phone could be used there. She realized she must have left it there after her game of fetch with her dog, Maf. She didn't want to think about that. She loved her little dog but she still hadn't come to terms with what had just happened outside. She was still unsure if it was real or imagined.

After Frank had given Maf to Marilyn, Patricia Newcomb had been one of the first to meet the new dog. Newcomb tried to hide her annoyance that Marilyn planned to tell everyone (especially Joe) that the dog had been a gift from her, and not Frank. She was happy to do something for Marilyn but did not want to encourage her relationship with Sinatra. When she asked about the dog's name, Marilyn said, "Mop." The little white fur ball resembled a mop top. "Mop?" Newcomb asked. Then poking fun at Sinatra's connection to Mafia figures, she exclaimed, "With hidden ties to Frank, you should call him Maf, Honey!" A few of the women in Marilyn's close social circle often called each other Honey, and Marilyn knew that's how she meant it, but decided to have a little fun of her own. "Maf Honey," Marilyn said, "Yes, that's it." Maf for short, the name stuck.

Margaux and Harlow. In more playful times this is what the dynamic duo, Margot Patricia Newcomb and Marilyn Monroe called each other. Newcomb preferred the fancier French spelling, Margaux. Newcomb had reappeared in Marilyn's life in late 1960, near the end of filming on the movie *The Misfits*, and had been a feature player in her life ever since. Not only Marilyn's press agent, she soon became a friend, companion, confidant and sometimes even, a kind of life manager.

The two had met when Newcomb briefly worked for Marilyn in 1956, during the filming of *Bus Stop*. There was a sexual tension between the two and Marilyn had to let her go. This tension is usually described as a "sexual rivalry," like they were both after the same man. But this is just before Marilyn's marriage to Arthur. The only rivalry may have been the one between Miller and Newcomb. Marilyn had become disenchanted with her "experiments" with women. Natasha, Crawford and Dietrich all let her unfulfilled. She was going in a decidedly different direction with her life and almost desperately wanted to build a family. There was no room for Newcomb in her life then, but now they were loyal friends. At least that's what Marilyn assumed.

What had Margaux done? Marilyn tried to put the pieces together. She was angry when her friend sided with Bobby over her. Her mind drifted back to earlier in the day. Marilyn peered out one of the front windows and looked out on the courtyard of her home. Bobby had just left and Newcomb was walking him out. The two stopped to talk. Peter raced ahead towards his car. Marilyn was furious. Flushed with anger, she had demanded RFK and Lawford leave her home. She almost had to physically kick them out. She was tired of being a pawn in some insane game between Frank and Bobby. She was sick of being passed around like a piece of meat, given no more regard than a side of beef. Bobby had been so free with his promises when he wanted something from her. Now he had come over and tried to barter between threats and demands.

Bobby had his back to Marilyn but she could see Newcomb clearly. Marilyn could read lips, a skill she acquired as a child when she would spend hours in movie theaters, intently watching the actors over and over. It came in handy because sometimes Marilyn had trouble hearing. Newcomb told Bobby, "Don't worry, I'll take care of it."

Marilyn wasn't really surprised by this. She knew Newcomb's infatuation with Bobby bordered on hero worship. It's what Marilyn saw next that surprised her. Just after Newcomb said she'd "take care of it," she discretely moved her hand towards Bobby's hand, just as Marilyn had done with Pat on the tarmac. Bobby reacted just as Pat had. He momentarily recoiled then he grabbed Newcomb's shoulders in much the same way Pat had grabbed both of Marilyn's hands. There was more to Newcomb's relationship with Bobby than Marilyn had ever suspected. "This explains so much," Marilyn said out loud to no one that could hear.

Marilyn found herself in her changing room. She looked around. How long had she been daydreaming? She wished the whole day had been a nightmare she could awake from. What was she doing? The phone. She needed a phone. She had left the main phone in the guest house and she would have to use her private line. Her private phone was on a long cord and could be carried around the house. She walked towards the phone, picked it up and brought it out into the hallway. She spotted Mrs. Murray and told her she decided against a drive and was going to turn in. She opened her bedroom door and then saw the last of Eunice Murray as she turned and wished her good night.

Marilyn brought the phone into her room and placed it on the bed along with the little slip of paper that had a Kennedy phone number on it. She then closed her bedroom door. The carpet was so thick that sometimes the phone cord would not go under the door. Trapped between the frame and door it would prevent the door from completely closing. That would be the case on this night and Marilyn either didn't realize or didn't care.

She was going to try and call one last time. Maybe fate would finally intervene. But first she wanted to hear Frank sing. Frank seemed so angry when she left Cal-Neva one week before. Would he even speak to her, let alone go through with the movie projects they had planned? It didn't matter now. She put on some records. Slowly swaying to the music, she slipped off her clothes. She sat on the bed and dialed the Hyannis Port number. She just wanted to talk to Pat, at least one last time. It seemed like an eternity and she lost count of how many times the phone rang but finally someone answered. Momentary elation quickly turned to despair as the person immediately hung up. Marilyn hid her face in her pillow as she began to cry.

The chloral hydrate acted even faster than she had anticipated. She felt she was on the verge of passing out. If the family wouldn't let her talk to Pat, then she would do the next best thing she could think of. She would say goodbye through Peter. She dialed the Lawford beach house. As the phone rang Marilyn thought of Bobby offering Peter as some kind of consolation prize. Telling her she could continue to see Peter and go to the beach house when Pat wasn't there. "Jerk!" Marilyn said out loud. Peter answered and seemed relieved to hear from her. He probably thought she had come to her senses and was going to come and do what Bobby had asked. After all Bobby had promised he could make the whole problem go away. All she had to do was give him the photo. But she wanted answers first.

Frank wanted her to destroy it. He had just wanted her to see it as some kind of wake up call. He may have been right, maybe she needed the help only a hospital could provide, but she also needed to know what was going on and why nobody would tell her what was happening.

But now, she was beyond all that. She was not going to capitulate to Bobby's demands unless he explained to her what was going on. The last times she had talked to Pat, both in person and on the phone, she told Marilyn they would have to do exactly what Bobby said and let him handle it. But when Marilyn refused his demands that afternoon he became angry, just as he had in New York. Did Pat know Bobby would forbid Marilyn to have contact with anyone in the Kennedy family, including her? Did Bobby know how devastating to Marilyn it would be to hear that?

On the phone Peter turned hyper when he couldn't understand Marilyn and tried to verbally slap her into a response he could understand. When she told him she had taken the last of her Nembutal he made a joke thinking she was just seeking attention or sympathy. Marilyn let him rant. She had called for just one reason, to get a message to Pat. It was the only thing on her mind. So when Peter paused, Marilyn said with as much clarity as she could still muster, "Tell Pat... tell Pat... always." Peter was almost yelling into the phone, "Marilyn. You're not making sense. Always what?"

Marilyn flashed back to the last time she saw Pat. They had talked on the phone since but Marilyn preferred to think of their last moment together, face to face, when Pat mouthed the word that meant so much, "Always."

"Always too," Marilyn said softly into the phone. Lawford bellowed, "Tell Pat always to what?" Marilyn had grown weary of Peter. She put the phone down on the bed and drifted away... But only for a moment. The squawk of an old crow awakened her. Lawford was still talking. When he stopped for a breath Marilyn let him know the conversation was over by saying, "Say goodbye to Pat... and say goodbye to the Prez...... and Charlie... say goodbye to yourself 'cause you're a nice guy." With that she put the phone down beside her on the bed and laid her head on her pillow. She had said the only important thing on her mind, the only thing that really mattered anymore, she had said goodbye to Pat.

Marilyn woke with a gasp. She would frequently wake with a fright, sometimes hours sometimes even just minutes after passing out. She couldn't judge how long it had been, she was still so very groggy. The light in the room was still on but it was quiet now. Too quiet. She had to have Frank with her, even if only his voice. She pulled her self up and shuffled to the record player. It was just then Mrs. Murray was coming into the house. She had been in the guest cottage putting the dog down for the night when she had received a phone call from Marilyn's lawyer Milton Rudin. He had inquired as to how Marilyn was doing and Eunice Murray had told him she was fine. He was rather insistent that she check so she was coming into the house to do just that.

When she reached Marilyn's room she was about to knock, but because of the phone cord, the door was slightly ajar and she could see movement in the room. Plus she heard the sound of the records beginning to play again. Murray turned and went back to the guest house to finish her call with Rudin. Marilyn stood alone, naked in her room, rocking back and forth to the sound of Frank's voice. When she turned to walk back to her bed she must have turned her head too quickly because she became lightheaded and stumbled backward into the door. The door knob struck her in the side as she tried unsuccessfully to catch her balance by leaning on the door. She crumbled, winching in pain, and tumbled to the floor. Knees bent, with her hips and lower torso against the door, she lay with her chest on the floor, her face buried in the thick carpet. She passed out and as she started to drift away, she began to dream... She is standing with Pat and Frank in his apartment... Peter has just left to find some juice... Witchcraft begins to play...

Part II

Before I begin Part II was this book, there is something I should probably explain about the story you just finished. When I originally wrote the book, the first chapter and the last few pages of the book contained Frank Sinatra song lyrics. Since I didn't have the money to pay for permission from the copyright holders, I had to remove them. The lyrics were an attempt to tie the beginning and the last half of the book together as a signal that much of what you just read was a death dream. Marilyn was reliving her connection to the Kennedys and how those relationships got her to that point on the evening of August 4, 1962. Much of the first half of the book was meant to be from the perspective of a narrator, given a glimpse of this death dream and trying to make sense of it. The way it was supposed to play out was that the narrator (me) would conduct an investigation on a website and in social media, then ultimately reveal what really happened. That's what I had planned. What happened in real life didn't work out that way at all.

I published the *Last Love* short story on February 14, 2017. It was meant as a Valentine for Marilyn fans. The response turned out to be like a grade school kid who goes to school on Valentines Day with a card for everyone then comes home empty-handed. My story was ignored.

As I said in the introduction to this book, I hoped it would spark debate, at which point I'd clarify and explain the story in a series of web posts on the site NormaJeane.xyz. I spent six months on Twitter promoting the book and couldn't get a single person to even comment on the book, let alone leave a review or ask questions. I vastly underestimated how leery the Marilyn community is of new claims of ground-breaking discoveries in the Marilyn case. I guess at this point it's better for them to just ignore new claims as just the ramblings of a crackpot, or the work of yet another sleazy self-promoter out to make a fast buck by exploiting Marilyn's popularity.

I should have known that would happen. I, like anyone else who has ever seriously considered this case, is highly skeptical of anyone who claims to have definitive answers to what happened on Fifth Helena on the night of August 4, 1962. There are just too many competing scenarios to consider. The most commonly agreed upon conclusion to Marilyn's death is that she committed suicide. So I thought I'd start with a story that included what now appears to be the most likely answer to the Marilyn mystery, that is, on that fateful Saturday night, Marilyn Monroe deliberately took her own life. She was telling everyone that had ever used, discarded and disappointed her that she had enough.

But what was it that pushed her over the edge? Why on that date and that time in her life, when everything was improving did she decide to die. I spoke earlier about contradictory facts where both appear to be true. One of the major dilemmas in the Marilyn mystery is the following paradox. Both these statement appear to be true:

1) Marilyn was not having an affair with Robert Kennedy, and

2) Marilyn killed herself because Robert Kennedy broke up with her and severed all ties between her and the Kennedy family.

Obviously both statements can't be true. But do they point to a greater truth? Did she have a deep, meaningful connection with a Kennedy that suddenly ended that night? A positive answer to that question might provide the elusive answer to the greatest Marilyn mystery. Why? Why would Marilyn choose to end her own life?

Perhaps I went wrong by declaring Marilyn's love for Pat Kennedy Lawford as sexual. I admit it's a hypothesis without much foundation in verifiable facts. But isn't that likely to be true in all secret love affairs? Especially one that would have been so socially shocking and inflammatory that disclosure and the public condemnation that followed would have ruined both of their lives, not to mention the effects it would have had on a powerful family and the president of the United States?

Couldn't this explain why the circumstances surrounding Marilyn's death had to be kept secret and were never talked about by the Kennedys, Sinatra and DiMaggio. Couldn't this explain DiMaggio's hatred for the whole family, and not just the brothers? And also explain why even after appeals from Marilyn's lawyer and housekeeper, he still barred Pat Kennedy Lawford from the funeral? I believe a strong love between the two woman is more than a possibility, it's actually a probability. So why make that bond sexual? Do I have any proof? Is there any proof of a sexual relationship between Marilyn Monroe and Pat Kennedy Lawford? To be totally honest, no, there's not one shred of solid evidence that the two were ever lovers. So, how can I speculate that the two were ever lovers? Because to me it made a lot sense, especially considering all the conflicting evidence I had acquired. It tied together a bunch of loose ends and finally explained why, after so many years and the murders of the brothers, did the Kennedy involvement in Marilyn's life still have to be kept such a big secret.

I don't expect you to just accept this conjecture as fact. I'll try to convince you with evidence. The two main resources that convinced me of the possibility of an affair between MM and PKL are two current and well respected biographies of Marilyn Monroe by Lois Banner and J. Randy Taraborrelli. My assumption of an affair is the result of a "marriage" of information presented in these two bio's. The first is Banner's, *The Passion and the Paradox*. Banner makes a convincing argument for Marilyn's bisexuality. The second is Taraborrelli's, *The Secret Life of Marilyn Monroe*. Taraborrelli reveals, for the first time in any biography, just how close the friendship between Marilyn Monroe and Pat Kennedy Lawford was. Taraborrelli gives us a glimpse of just how intimate the two were by relaying never before offered testimony from one of Pat's friends, Pat Brennan. I think the most relevant piece of information is in an appendix. It's in the back of the book where he tells us that Pat Brennan stated the Pat Kennedy Lawford was never the same after the Cal-Neva weekend, and that this time period marked the end of the Lawford marriage.

There are several other "clues" that seem to support my conclusion. It's been reported that Pat and Peter Lawford slept in separate bedrooms. Even their son Christopher repeats the well worn rumor in his book that his mother made the sign of the cross before sex with his father. It's said that marriage wasn't in her nature and that she married and had children because that's what was expected of Kennedy women. Pat tolerated Peter's extramarital activities and only balked when one of his trollops had the audacity to call the house. Pat was the first Kennedy to get a divorce, something which was taboo not only in her family but also in her religion. She never remarried after divorcing Peter, and there is no indication that she was ever involved with another man for the rest of her life. I will admit that none of that is proof. The way I presented this affair in *Last Love* is as a kind of death dream on Marilyn's part as she drifts off into oblivion. It's presented as the way she saw the last months unfold. I admit all my "evidence" is in reality a very flimsy foundation to base such an assumption. But it's something to consider and that was the purpose of Part I of this book, to convince people there is more to the story of Marilyn's death and that there are new avenues left to investigate.

Rumors that Marilyn was lesbian by nature date back to her lifetime and constitute parts of the earliest conspiracy theories as evidenced by the 1964 FBI file titled "Robert F Kennedy." We will consider that document later. A statement by Dr. Greenson that Marilyn wasn't involved with any men at the time of her death may be a clue that she was involved with a women. Ultimately, it may be unimportant if the two women were actual lovers. If Marilyn felt she was being "cut off" from the Kennedy family and that meant losing a dear and valued friend it would have been very upsetting for her. That kind of rejection, especially after being told by Pat, "You're a Kennedy now," would have been devastating for someone who all her life longed to be part of a family and who had such adverse reactions to rejection. It would also explain why in her last phone call with Peter Lawford, the first person she wanted to say goodbye to was Pat.

I think this whole issue is important because it speaks to Marilyn's state of mind on the evening of her death. The purpose of this book is to stimulate discussion about Marilyn's demise and offer new avenues of investigation. Monroe was an important figure in 20th century history and she deserves better than how her story has devolved over the years. There are untapped clues to the circumstances of her last month which contributed to her death. We will begin to consider those clues by examining two of the seven keys I introduced earlier, the Kennedy Connection, and the Lesbian Rumors.

THE KENNEDY CONNECTION

A consensus among Marilyn researchers about topics such as her childhood, her career, her love life, her mental condition and a host of others is hard to come by. So controversy about her death is likely to never go away. (Unless, of course, her killer confesses.)

Monroe's connection to John Kennedy and his family is only one aspect of her life that biographers disagree about. But it's one where you find the most extreme polarities. Her relationship with JFK is either presented as "much ado about nothing" or the steamiest, most scandalous love affair of the 20th century. Rarely is there a middle ground. Someday in the future, a competent, rational historian, without a left or right wing political bias and without an agenda to either bash or defend the Kennedys, will turn their attention to writing a Marilyn biography. I feel that if that were to happen, the results of this historians findings about Marilyn's connection to JFK, would look something like this:

- In the 1950s, Marilyn Monroe and John Kennedy crossed paths on one documented occasion. (April In Paris Ball, 1957) It's possible the two may have both been present at party or two in Los Angeles in that time period, but documentation is lacking. With almost certainty, there was no affair dating back to the 1950s.

- Details of the first time they met, with the two of them together in room, having a discussion and getting to know each other, is lost to history. It most likely happened in the spring of 1960, the same time period Monroe began a friendship with Pat Kennedy Lawford. There is a reliable witness who observed Monroe and JFK walking on the beach near the Lawford home in the months before the Democratic National Convention. JFK spent a lot of time in Los Angeles campaigning, so it's likely he met Marilyn at that time, at a Lawford social event.

Because it's confirmed by Kennedy insiders and loyalists, it's likely Monroe was present on the last day of the convention. But even this isn't a proven fact. It's very curious that with the abundance of press and TV coverage, and with all the photos of Pat Lawford with Frank Sinatra and his "Pack", that there isn't a single photo of Marilyn being present. Perhaps she didn't make it to the convention, but arrived in town in time to go to the after party at the Lawfords. Stories of her showing up to this party escorted by Sammy Davis, Jr, have a ring of truth to them. The tales of Marilyn meeting JFK at Puccini's are most likely garbled accounts of a future encounter or are completely fabricated. Conclusion: Marilyn and JFK's relationship in mid 1960 was most likely social and platonic.

- For the remainder of 1960 through the fall of 1961 there appears to be no contact at all between the two. It wasn't until September, after Marilyn returned to live in LA, strengthened a friendship with Pat Lawford and was in a relationship with Frank Sinatra, that Kennedy and Monroe crossed paths again.

- Given confirmation of witnesses within Kennedy circles, it likely Marilyn was in Washington and possibly at Hyannis Port in the fall of 1961. But she was with Frank Sinatra, and she was there as a friend of Pat, so a Monroe/JFK affair at this time seems unlikely.

- It was in Oct/Nov 1961 that the relationship between Monroe and JFK turned flirtatious. Given the reputation of the two, this seems inevitable; at least the rumors would be. The reason for the flirtation appears to be because Sinatra was pulling away from Monroe. In this time period Marilyn was seen at a Democratic fundraiser in Los Angeles in which JFK was present. She was also at one or two social events at the Lawford home in Santa Monica when JFK was there. A reliable Secret Service agent from Kennedy's team remembers Marilyn being there when JFK made an impromptu swim in the ocean, where he was instantly mobbed by an adoring public. Even at this point a sexual relationship with JFK is unlikely because every time the two were together, it was in the presence of Marilyn's close friend, Pat Lawford. That would not change until February 1962. Of note here, JFK living up to his reputation as a millionaire playboy surely by now must be considered a historical certainty. On the other hand, while she was no virginal saint, Monroe's sexually promiscuity has been grossly exaggerated.

  - If Monroe and Kennedy had an affair that went beyond a one night fling at Bing Crosby's, it likely started in February 1962 at the Fifi Fell party and continued sporadically until it ended at Crosby's. This "affair" may have been more than once, but couldn't have been much more than four isolated occurrences. This number accounts for the rumors of meetings at the Carlyle hotel in NY and the Fontainebleau in

Miami (both highly questionable). Whatever the extent of this "affair," it doesn't appear to have meant that much to either one of them. Marilyn wasn't stupid, it's highly doubtful she could have ever been so delusional that she actually believed either Kennedy brother would divorce their wife and marry her. That said, it does appear she revealed her and JFK's intimacy to a few close friends, and it's likely she was hurt by an off hand comment by JFK about her "not being first lady material." Like all Kennedy affairs it probably meant more to his handlers (including RFK) who had to keep his extramarital excursions secret.

- By April 1962, the Marilyn/JFK fling would be over. The two would meet one more time (platonically) at the presidents birthday gala.

So there you have it. That would be the competent, rational historians conclusions. And then there's my version. While you might find the "twist" of my story questionable, and probably even unbelievable, I'll still ask you to consider it possible. What I hope you take away from the *Last Love* story is that the most significant relationship Marilyn had with a Kennedy was with Patricia Kennedy Lawford. But was that relationship sexual?

It really shouldn't matter. Believe it or not, I find the whole matter distasteful. Not because of any condemnation on my part, I'm a strong defender of "love is love," I find it distasteful because it shouldn't matter. A person's sex life should be a private matter. For many people, their sexuality isn't something that's easily definable. Sexuality is often fluid and doesn't conform to labels. If I didn't think it was relevant to her death I wouldn't bring it up at all. But it is not only relevant, I believe it's crucial to sort out the lesbian rumors before we can make a determination of how and why Marilyn died. That said, we can now turn to the next "key."

LESBIAN RUMORS

At first glance, considering Marilyn Monroe a lesbian seems like revisionist history projecting a modern issue back into the past. But lesbian rumors go all the way back to Marilyn's lifetime. The lesbian rumors are relevant to a discussion of Marilyn's death because they are so closely correlated to the first conspiracy theories. Author Ezra Goodman was making claims as early as 1963 that he had uncovered information that Marilyn was "dabbling with lesbianism" toward the end of her life.

The rumors began life while Marilyn was alive. They started early in her career when she briefly lived with her acting coach, Natasha Lytess. Natasha herself is likely the source of many of those rumors because of comments she made about Marilyn at the time. Further confirmation of their sexual intimacy comes from the lighthearted ribbing that Frank Sinatra gave Joe DiMaggio about the Lytess/Monroe relationship. The whole wrong-door-raid may have been a result of this ribbing in an attempt to catch Marilyn in the act with a woman. This was revealed by sources close to Sinatra. For some reason, DiMaggio thought that a public revelation of an affair would bring Marilyn back to his arms. If his goal was to end her career, bringing a lesbian affair to the attention of the public would do the trick. Hal Schaefer says the affair they almost uncovered was with him.

Marilyn's affair with Lytess may have been nothing more than experimentation, but who can say for sure. Lytess, around the time of Marilyn's death, would write a booking confirming the affair. It was never fully published and only pieces of her manuscript have become public knowledge. The pieces that she did make public in interviews were very carefully worded to insinuate an affair without actually confirming it. It's almost as if she had agreed not to reveal the affair but still wanted the public to know the truth. I find this fact interesting. Lytess was dying of cancer at the time and was facing huge medical bills. Publishing her "tell all" book would have been very lucrative at a time she desperately needed money. The question that forms in my mind is: Who, or what family, would have a vested interest in the book *not* being published and would also have the financial ability to pay her *not* to publish? I think you know where I'm going with this. If Marilyn was having an affair with Pat Kennedy Lawford, the family would want any rumors of Marilyn dabbling in lesbianism kept quiet. Like her relationship with the Kennedys, the MCA case and the events at Cal-Neva, there was a concerted effort to downplay or ignore these very important parts of Marilyn's last year.

Other lesbian rumors concerning Joan Crawford and Marlene Dietrich originated while Marilyn was alive. In the case of Joan Crawford, this rumor was even possibly confirmed by Marilyn herself. Other rumors that began circulation after her death concerning Lili St Cyr, Betty Grable, Judy Garland, Elizabeth Taylor and Bridget Bardot are most certainly revisionist history with no basis in reality.

There are other rumors that date back to Marilyn's lifetime. One concerns Marilyn and her publicist Pat Newcomb. In Monroe's final months the two were almost inseparable. Pat was working closely with Marilyn during the week, then spent weekends with her at her house. People began to talk. This is confirmed by a co-worker of Newcomb's at the Arthur Jacobs agency.

There is also another rumor that was revealed in Anthony Summers' book *Goddess*. He doesn't give an exact date for this. His only clue as to when it happened is that he places this story after he had just been speaking of events which occurred in the fall of 1961. He tells of a woman who had to be paid off because she was about to reveal information of an affair with Monroe. This is how he describes it in his book:

"In the same period, the consultants were used to smooth over a bizarre matter involving a Hollywood woman who claimed to have had a lesbian encounter with Marilyn and who seemed likely to brag about it. The woman was silenced with a cash payment, though the facts of the matter were never resolved." (Source: A. Summers, *Goddess*)

That's all he says about this tantalizing tidbit and he doesn't provide a source for it in his end notes. I'd like you to keep this story in mind as I tell you about another one. This story is found in a recently revealed document from the FBI concerning a Hollywood woman named Lulu Porter. Before we consider the FBI file, lets examine any possible connection between Porter and Monroe. There is no record in any biography that they knew each other, but could they have crossed paths? As we saw, Summers places this story in the last year of Marilyn's life. What dominated that time period was negotiation for, then the filming of, *Somethings Got to Give*. Bob Mackie designed costumes for Marilyn for her role as Ellen Arden in the unfinished film *SGTG*. Mackie was gay and in later years would live with his life partner Ray Aghayan. But at this period in his life he was married to Lulu Porter.

Most of the files the FBI provides about Marilyn were released in the 1990's. Almost all the information that the FBI shares is from informants, tipsters and press clippings. Most of it is nothing more than hearsay and gossip. That said, there is still important information that can retrieved from these files. The file I'm about to discuss, titled "Robert F. Kennedy", didn't surface until about a decade ago. We know it's authentic because after it's disclosure the FBI added it to their Marilyn Monroe files on the FBI website. The file appears to be the results of one of the first independent investigations into Monroe's death. Most current commentators dismiss the file.

Since was written to the FBI in 1964 with claims of a Monroe/RFK affair, many claim it to be from Frank Capell, the man who wrote what's considered the first conspiracy book. I doubt this to be the case. There are many internal inconsistencies between the two works. Probably the most significant is that the author of the FBI letter claims the drug that killed Marilyn was the barbiturate Seconal. Capell knew it was Nembutal. Capell also knew the correct spelling of Pat Newcomb's name, while the FBI document has an alternate spelling, Newcombe. There are similarities between Capell's book and the FBI document, but there are enough differences to make it unlikely that they came from the same source. Unless the FBI leaked the information to Capell and he cleaned up the errors.

What's relevant to this discussion are the references to lesbian affairs. Capell doesn't come out and say that Monroe and Newcomb were intimate but he does imply it. In his book, Capell quotes Goodman about Marilyn "dabbling with lesbianism" late in life, and in a section about Newcomb he writes:

"At the time of Marilyn's death Pat lived at 120 South Canon Drive, Beverly Hills, California, and frequently stayed overnight with Marilyn. Pat is now in her thirty's and has remained single. It is no secret in Hollywood and Beverly Hills that Pat and Marilyn were very close and that, while Marilyn had male interests mainly, Pat was not given to romantic interests in men." (Source: *The Strange Death of Marilyn Monroe*, Frank Capell)

It should be pointed out that Capell is a lying nut job that see's everything through an "every leftist is a commie" lens. He was actually indicted for making untrue, homosexual smears against a politician. There are many inaccuracies in his book and he could be way off base on this. Fred Guiles was an author who worked closely with Newcomb on his screenplay, turned magazine article, turned book, *Norma Jean*. In that book he says that Pat was briefly married before working with Marilyn. I could find no other documentation of this marriage. Newcomb did marry (again?), although it was late in life. There is evidence to suggest Newcomb did "love" a man at this time. If that love was romantic or merely hero worship, only Newcomb can say. Was that love so strong that she would kill to protect this man's reputation is also a question that you will have to ask Pat. That man, by the way, is Robert F. Kennedy. Jeanne Martin, the wife of Dean Martin implied Newcomb carried a torch for RFK for many years. Rupert Allan also made a comment that indicated Newcomb was interested in Bobby. My purpose in including quotes from Capell's book is to investigate things that were being said at the time, not to substantiate them.

Now lets consider the three page letter sent to the FBI in 1964. The author considers the Monroe/RFK affair a known fact. The theory that's set forth in this letter is that Monroe was induced to commit suicide. Several people are involved in this conspiracy including Newcomb. The letter states:

"It is reported the housekeeper and Marilyn's personal secretary and press agent, Pat Newcombe, were cooperating in the plan to induce suicide. Pat Newcombe was rewarded by her cooperation by being put on the Federal payroll..." (Source: Marilyn Monroe FBI file, FBI website)

For the first page and a half of the letter to the FBI, the author develops this scenario right up to the call from Joe DiMaggio Jr, on the evening of Monroe's death. Then the author abruptly changes topics. For one small paragraph he jumps to one year later and includes a few sentences about Pat Newcomb, along with White House press secretary, Pierre Salinger, picking Lulu Porter to represent the U.S. in a foreign festival.

After that strange, seeming unrelated news, he starts a new paragraph whose topic is a lesbian affair. That paragraph starts with this sentence:

"Marilyn was as also having an intermittent lesbian affair with XXXXXXXX

XXXXXXXXXXXXXXXXXXXXXXXXXXXX." (Source: FBI file)

The X's in the above excerpt represent a portion of the text that has been redacted. It's much longer than just a name. It would be very interesting to find out exactly who is being referred to. My hunch is that it's a name with a further identifying characteristic. Could it be something like this: Patricia Lawford, sister of the president? At first glance this may seem highly improbable. So what would lead me to make such an outrageous assumption? Allow me to explain. The next sentence in the FBI letter is about JFK coming out to California for sex parties. The rest of the letter is devoted to details of the Kennedy involvement in the cover up of the circumstances that led to the death of Marilyn Monroe. We have a three page letter outlining a conspiracy involved in Marilyn's death. In the middle of this document are parts about Lulu Porter, and that information is immediately followed by the lesbian affair line. Both subjects seem oddly out of place. In the authors mind they must both be relevant to the theme of he letter, which is there was Kennedy involvement in the death of Marilyn Monroe.

There is a precedent for Pat Kennedy's names showing up in FBI files which detail the sexual escapades of the family. I'm speaking of a document that can be found in Ted Kennedy's FBI file. This one comes from the east coast and has received some notoriety. Because of it's salacious content, many Marilyn authors have commented on it. It involves orgies at the Carlyle Hotel in New York. When it was first released in the 1990's it had several names blacked out. When it was re-released online in 2012, one of the names on the list that had been redacted was now visible, it was Mrs Peter Lawford. But what does Pat Kennedy have to do with a singer selected for a foreign film festival? Is there anything that connects Pat Kennedy Lawford to Lulu Porter? For that answer let's take a closer look at Lulu Porter.

It turns out that this letter to the FBI is correct about Porter being selected by Pierre Salinger to represent the United States in a cultural exchange program with Poland. Pat Newcomb, in her role with the U.S. Information Agency is also involved. Lulu Porter wasn't well known at the time. She was very young. She had never made a record and wasn't even known as a singer, she was just another Hollywood starlet. She had only been in one movie, *The Brass Bottle*, and in that she did not sing, she did a belly dance. Her appearances on television had been limited to a few local stations. So when she was selected to represent the United States it raised some eyebrows and reporters naturally inquired how it was that she was chosen.

She admitted that she never auditioned for the State Department and she claimed she didn't know (or wouldn't tell) why she was chosen, but she does offer up an explanation for how.

What follows in quotes is from the August 6, 1963 issue of the Pittsburgh Post-Gazette:

"Miss Porter has only one clue to explain her selection. This was an event that occurred in April or May. At that time she was singing in a small nightclub in Beverly Hills, Ye Little Club. She had won an audition there that eventually brought her a five-week engagement. One night, after she finished her 25-minute act doing nine songs with a three-piece combo, she was congratulated by Pierre Salinger, President Kennedy's press secretary."

This was not a single story in one newspaper. It was an UPI story that was picked up by local papers. On the same date the Kansas City Times runs a similar story but includes quotes from her manager, who says,"the first he knew about the Polish festival was in June. I found a message to call the State Department."

As for why Miss Porter was awarded this "plum" assignment the articles states: "Miss Porter's manager, Jerry Fonarow, filled in a few gaps in Miss Porter's success story without being able to solve the mystery of his client's selection as the U. S. representative of pop singing. Fonarow 'discovered' Miss Porter the night she auditioned at Ye Little club, where he did publicity."

So is there any reason to connect this story with Pat Kennedy Lawford? The Post-Gazette article goes on to reveal there was someone with Salinger and Newcomb the evening they "discovered" Porter in the nightclub:

"Salinger had been at the club with one of the President's sisters, Mrs. Peter Lawford, and Pat

Newcomb, Marilyn Monroe's press agent at the time of her death." (Source: Pittsburgh Post-Gazette, August 6, 1963)

Now that a connection of Pat Kennedy Lawford to the Lulu Porter story has been established lets return the FBI letter. Immediately following the information about Porter comes the line about Marilyn's lesbian affair. It's reasonable to assume the author felt the two were connected. Who Marilyn was having an affair with has been redacted. The name probably wasn't Lulu Porter or Pat Newcomb because their names were not redacted in the preceding sentences. Besides Salinger, Newcomb and Porter the only other person publicly connected to this story is Mrs Peter Lawford. With that established, is there anything that connects the Porter incident to a lesbian rumor? I believe there is.

Before I began the section about the FBI letter, I asked you to keep in mind the small tidbit of information that Summers reveals about a pay-off to a woman who had an affair with Marilyn and was likely to brag about it. My working theory is that the woman Summers is referring to is Lulu Porter. My hunch is that Porter had been paid off while Marilyn was alive, but after Monroe's death she knew she was sitting on a major story and wanted more. Perhaps she felt like Marilyn had felt early in her career when she didn't want money, she wanted to be wonderful. Lulu may have been more interested in a big break, the kind of publicity that could kick start her lack luster career. It may be that Pat Newcomb and Pat Kennedy were instrumental in orchestrating that big break. Is there any proof this was a payoff. For that answer let me direct you to the online John F. Kennedy archives.

This information is available online for anyone that's interested to read it. It's an interview of Lucius Battle conducted in 1968 by Larry Hackman. Battle served as Assistant Secretary of State for Education and Culture and worked in some sort of oversight capacity of the program that sent Porter to Poland. The interview is available in the archives under the title, "Third of Three Oral History Interviews." I'm going to provide an excerpt of the interview below. I want you to notice how Battle appears to be a little tongue tied in his answer and how he chooses his words very carefully. Battle is answering questions about press criticism of the program. The program had received bad press a few times but there was only once it had received some flak from within the government. Here's a portion of Battle's response to the issue of press criticism:

"BATTLE...We got no really bad publicity after that, except there (sic) case involving Pierre Salinger [Pierre E.G. Salinger] that got a lot of low flak at the time. It involved—I can't remember the details of it—it involved a singer named Lulu Porter, I think was her name. Glen Lipscomb is the one I mentioned that objected to Jesse Unruh. He was the one also who got on this particular girl who went to some competition which she won. She had some sort of—she wasn't given grant by us, as I remember, but she was given facilitative service, but had the blessing. It was done in a way that I felt.... It was when I was in Bogotá because I read it in the press when I landed in Miami; that's the first time I'd heard of it. And this caused a great deal of flak because Pierre Salinger was given credit for—he and Pat Newcomb were given credit for having selected her at a night-club they'd gone to. And I do not recall, my recollection is that the case, it was a borderline case, where we had not done much to help but we had given some sort of facilitative assistance. It never should have occurred; it was very bad, but it wasn't disastrous. We got a little criticism on that one, but that's about the only one that I can recall that we got any flak on." (Source: JFK Library website)

So she received a "facilitative service." Is that government speak for a bribe to keep her mouth shut?

All the information I've provided is all interesting, but I know it's not conclusive. There is nothing that can be definitively said about the rumors of Marilyn and lesbianism. Lois Banner has made the strongest case for Marilyn's bisexuality. I don't want to rehash ground that has already been covered. I want to examine why the rumors are so closely tied to the earliest murder theories. Ten years after Marilyn's death, in a rare interview, Dr Greenson would reveal that Marilyn was not involved with a man at the time of her death. Was he implying that she was involved with a woman? I developed the theme as a way to provide some rational explanation of why Marilyn Monroe may have committed suicide. Through all the years of research I put into this case, the only explanation that makes sense to me, is that Marilyn had some sort of relationship with Robert Kennedy. For some reason, on that last weekend of her life, she was trying to reach him. His reaction to her trying to reach him, was to either ignore her or to have harsh words with her, on the phone or in person. Her reaction to his actions was to first get angry, then despondent. As the evening went on she grew more and more despondent over being cut off. The rejection she felt was instrumental in the decision to take her own life. But does this scenario really fit the facts? Is it reasonable to assume that a man she only met in person a handful of times could have had that effect her? It just doesn't seem likely.

People who like to downplay the role of the Kennedys in Marilyn's death do it by downplaying the role of the Kennedys in her life. Claims that Marilyn only met JFK four times are untenable. It almost had to be more than four. But whether it was four, six, ten or dozen it really doesn't matter. It may have been a brief affair, it may have been nothing much more than a flirtation, whatever it was, it was over months before her death. The situation with Bobby is different. She really did only meet him a handful of times. The reasons she called him over the summer I explained in *Last Love*. Marilyn's contact with RFK can be easily explained by three factors. First was the movie he was making with Fox. The second reason was the MCA case, and the third was for help with her studio. Short phone calls and a few face to face meetings with groups of people around doesn't sound like a romance. So how could his rejection have impacted her so deeply. It just doesn't make sense. What does make some sense is that being cut off from the entire family, in essence, was the same as being rejected by Pat Kennedy. And if Pat was someone she had finally made a deep and emotional bond with, this might have made her so despondent she felt like giving up. If Marilyn spent much of her life with a dark inner voice that told her she was worthless, this rejection may have been the final proof that voice was right.

The suicide scenario is just a theory. It's based on a whole bunch of conjecture and supposition. It definitely wouldn't satisfy anyone who demands hard evidence before reaching any conclusions. Perhaps the answer to the Marilyn mystery lies beyond the accidental overdose or suicide assumptions. Maybe we should look at alternate death scenarios for the answer. Are there other possibles that fit the forensic evidence? I believe there are, and that's where we shall turn our attention soon. But first, we need to look into the drugs that were found in Marilyn's system on the night she died.

THE DRUGS THAT KILLED MARILYN MONROE

NEMBUTAL:

The two major categories of sedative-hypnotics (anxiety/sleeping pills) are barbiturates and benzodiazepines. The chemical structure of the drugs in these groups are similar. In the 1950's and early 60's, barbiturates were routinely prescribed as a sleep-inducer. The most well known were Seconal (secobarbital) and Nembutal (pentobarbital). They were very common and if you lived at the time you would have frequently seen ads for these drugs in newspapers and magazines. Nembutal was even marketed as a sleep aid for children. They were routinely handed out to anyone who went to a doctor with the complaint of not being able to sleep. They were also used to treat anxiety.

At that time, benzodiazepines were relatively new and thus less common. In the years following Marilyn's death, this situation would reverse. Benzodiazepines would eventually replace barbiturates as the most commonly prescribed sedatives. The most well known examples of benzodiazepines are Valium and Librium.

Today, the pentobarbital that killed Monroe has few medical uses in humans. It's used by veterinarians to euthanize animals. In Europe (and where it's legal in the US,) it's also used in physician-assisted suicide.

Barbiturates depress the brain's electrical activity. They work within brain tissue to reduce the firing of neurons. Barbs slow down brain function and put the brain to sleep. With too many, breathing is suppressed and the heart stops pumping as hard, leading eventually to death.

CHLORAL HYDRATE

The chloral hydrate has always received very little attention when discussing the circumstances of Marilyn's death. Nembutal has always been the star in this show and always gets top billing. If anyone had paid attention to the chloral hydrate, we might not have had over five decades of controversy surrounding Marilyn's death. Any real investigation into Marilyn's death should have uncovered where Monroe got this drug that contributed to her untimely demise. The chloral hydrate is important because no one can definitively say where it came from. And the fact that there was never an investigation into where the drug came from goes a long way towards proving there was a cover-up so the true circumstances of Monroe's death would never be revealed.

So let's take a look at why this drug is so important for answering questions about how and why Marilyn died. Chloral hydrate has been around for a long time. When first synthesized it was classified as a hypnotic. Hypnos is Greek for sleep, so hypnotic is a fancy way to say sleeping aid. Since it can be used to control anxiety it's also considered a sedative. It was one of the first sedatives and was available long before barbiturates. By the mid 1800's it could be found in all the best asylums. It was the go-to sleep aid because it could knock a person out fast. It's dissolves easily in liquids, which is why it became they drug of choice in "Mickey Finn" concoctions. Legend has it that Mickey Finn was a saloon keeper in early 1900's Chicago, who would use knock-out drops (chloral hydrate) to drug and rob his customers.

If you are trying to die, or want to kill someone, mixing chloral hydrate with another sedative is a good way to do it. When mixed, the two are said to increase the effects of each other. Anna Nicole Smith died of an accidental overdose after mixing chloral hydrate with a sedative. The Jonestown mass suicides involved drinking Flavor Aid (a soft drink beverage) poisoned with a mixture of drugs that included chloral hydrate and a sedative. The two are often used together today in physician assisted suicides. Chloral hydrate is a sedative-hypnotic drug that does not fit either major category of sedatives. It isn't a barbiturate or a benzodiazepine. So to say Marilyn died of acute barbiturate poisoning isn't technically correct. She died of a combination of sedative-hypnotic drugs.

Most of the conversation regarding Marilyn's death focuses mainly on the Nembutal. The amount of Nembutal in Monroe's system is always called a lethal dose. Sometimes the amount of chloral hydrate found in Monroe's system is also called a lethal dose, sometimes it's not. Even the coroner in charge of Marilyn's case uses conflicting statements concerning whether it was a lethal or toxic dose. Chloral hydrate became a confusing element of the Monroe case right from the beginning. The first toxicology report from the coroner's office on August 6, 1962, doesn't even mention chloral hydrate. Initially the only tests requested from the autopsy surgeon listed on the first toxicology report were for ethanol (alcohol) and barbiturates. On the first toxicology report only the blood was tested. Alcohol was absent and the barbiturate level was 4.5 mg. per cent. Since a level of 1.5 mg% can kill a person, it was said there was enough drugs in her system to kill 3 people. That can be misleading because Monroe's tolerance level was probably much higher than an average person. The amount found in her system was high, but no where near as high as what would be indicated by the hyperbole that would develop. Stories such as "there were enough drugs in her system to put down a heard of buffalo" or "enough to kill 15 people" are simply ridiculous and misleading.

One week after the first toxicology report, a second supplemental report was issued on August 13, 1962. This one reported that the blood contained 8 mg% of chloral hydrate. It also stated that a 13 mg% level of pentobarbital was found in the liver. What these numbers mean has been a source of constant debate ever since. Most "official" estimates of the number of pills Monroe took on the night of her death have been in the 40-50 range. Modern science says those initial estimates were too high. In this work I'm going to use the recent estimates of renowned forensic pathologist, Dr Cyril Wecht, who says the numbers indicate Monroe took 5 chloral hydrates and 12-24 Nembutal capsules.

All early sources reference Dr Engelberg as having prescribed Marilyn the Nembutal. Engelberg himself revealed this to the authorities. Confusion soon developed over how many and when these were prescribed. Was it 50 or 25? (It turned out to be two prescriptions for 25.) Was the second a refill or a new prescription? When was the first prescription filled? Those question's are a little harder to answer, you'll find sources with conflicting information. The only thing clear is that Dr Engelberg gave Marilyn what he calls a refill on August 3, 1962 for 25 capsules of Nembutal, but the vial itself appears to be an original prescription and not a refill. This anomaly has always led to the question of whether Monroe had enough Nembutal on hand to account for the levels found in her system. Following Marilyn's death, Dr Greenson is quoted as saying he did not know about this Nembutal prescription. Greenson says he turned over all prescription related duties to Engelberg, and the internist was supposed to notify him if he prescribed Marilyn Nembutal. Greenson and Engelberg were said to be coordinating in an effort to decrease her reliance on pills. Greenson reportedly had instructed Engelberg to switch her to a milder sedative. Librium was found on Marilyn's nightstand and I believe this is the milder sedative Engelberg had been prescribing during the months before Monroe's death. With all this attention on the Nembutal, it never seemed to occur to anyone to ask, "Who prescribed the chloral hydrate?" Since Dr Greenson had prescribed Marilyn chloral hydrate during the filming of *The Misfits*, it's often assumed he was the one to prescribe it. It wouldn't even become an issue until the LA District Attorney reopened the case in 1982. By this time Greenson had died, and only Engelberg was left to answer when the question was finally raised. Back in 1962, multiple prescriptions of different kinds were found on Monroe's nightstand. It seems at that time, anything that hadn't come from Engelberg was assumed to have come from Dr Lee Siegel, the Fox studio doctor. But in 1982 Siegel denied prescribing the chloral hydrate, and Engelberg said he hadn't prescribed it either. Engelberg didn't believe Greenson had given it to her and he assumed no doctor in the US would have still prescribed it. He assumed she had got it in Mexico, and that's the story he would maintain in all future interviews. This issue was never resolved and it goes a long way towards proving there never was a serious investigation of this case. Not in 1962, nor again in 1982.

Fast forward to the modern internet age. Within the last 20 years there has been an intense interest in Marilyn memorabilia. Anything even remotely associated with the icon continues to find it's way onto online auctions. Every scrap of paper that was ever in the vicinity of Monroe has been photographed, cataloged and sold online. Included in this vast assortment of ephemera are actual copies of prescriptions from Marilyn's last summer. One of those prescriptions just so happens to be one for chloral hydrate, and it's from Dr Engelberg! "Liar, liar, pants on fire," came the cry from the Marilyn community. It was said that, "Engelberg had been lying and here's the proof." Unfortunately for Engelberg, he was no longer alive to answer his critics. New documentaries were produced charging Engelberg with medical negligence. Engelberg took his place in the Marilyn "blame game," among such notable villains as, JFK, RFK, Greenson, Murray, Hoover, Hoffa, Castro, the FBI, the CIA, Giancana and a couple of thugs named Needles and Mugsy; and even our reptilian overloads. Was the blame warranted? Things are rarely cut and dry in the Monroe case. Researching Marilyn is like being sucked into a black hole that leads to a vortex of contradictions, wrapped around a riddle, who's center is an enigma. There is never easy answers, and this piece of evidence ultimately leads to more questions. What do I mean? If you do an image search online for Engelberg, Monroe, prescription and Librium, you will be led to a photo of another prescription from that summer. This one is an Engelberg prescription for Librium. This is the drug I believe Greenson had switched Marilyn to when he came back from his vacation in June, when he began to coordinate with Engelberg to reduce Monroe's dependence on pills. This is an "official" Engelberg prescription, complete with his name and the address of his practice at the top. Now do an image search with these search terms: chloral hydrate, Engelberg, Monroe and prescription. You should find a chloral hydrate prescription from Engelberg dated June 1962. Compare this prescription with the one for Librium. The unmistakable conclusion from this comparison is that the handwriting doesn't match! The Engelberg signatures on each document aren't the least bit similar. How can this anomaly be explained. Three possible explanations are: the prescriptions are fakes, someone forged Engelberg's signature or the prescriptions were phoned into the pharmacy. But even this last possibility doesn't prove they were phoned in my Engelberg, it could have been someone masquerading as Engelberg. The Nembutal in Marilyn's system was enough to kill her and it's clear it was prescribed by Engelberg. Why would he lie about the chloral hydrate? This new evidence throws a curve ball into the investigation of Marilyn's death. It requires new theories to accommodate this information. What follows are two new scenarios concerning Marilyn's last summer that try to explain where the mystery prescriptions came from and the part they played in her death.

ALTERNATIVE DEATH SCENARIO:
UNINTENTIONAL HOMICIDE

I'd like to remind everyone from the start that this is a hypothetical reconstruction of events that took place 55 years ago. It's offered as a scenario, just one possible way to make sense of the documentary evidence that has been left to us. It's important to remember that people are innocent until proven guilty. I don't want anyone to go vigilante on the women in this scenario. It's easy, and a bit cowardly to accuse people of crimes after they are dead and can't defend themselves. I would rather do this while the offending parties are still alive so they can speak in their own defense.

It's probably pointless to say that this new evidence demands an investigation by the police. Given the failed attempts to open a "real" investigation in the past I know that's not likely to happen. Those attempts in the past were never taken seriously because the people proposing them were mainly charlatans, fame seekers or they were just plain greedy and willing to lie to sell a story. I know you've heard it all before. Every few years now, for over half a century, new claims are offered up as groundbreaking discoveries. Can this one be any different? I believe it is. Evidence that Dr Greenson nor Dr Engelberg gave Marilyn a prescription for the chloral hydrate that killed her must be considered and explained.

So... lets resume the story that was laid out in Part I by going back to the time period of early June 1962. For everyone who can't accept the premise offered in *Last Love* of a sexual relationship between Pat Kennedy and Marilyn Monroe, please feel free to assume that they were just close, intimate friends.

This scenario begins the weekend following Marilyn's birthday on June 1, 1962. Marilyn is deeply upset. Henry Weinstein, the producer of Monroe's last unfinished film, *Something's Got to Give* got to know Marilyn very well in her last months. He is convinced that whatever happened that weekend was more important than the weekend she died. He's quoted as saying, "Something happened that weekend and what it was nobody knows. I think the only one who really knew what happened is Pat Newcomb." Maybe he was trying to tell us something.

Marilyn's shrink was out of town and had been for weeks. Her internist Dr Engelberg, was also unavailable. Greenson had been Marilyn's psychiatrist since she moved from New York back to California in mid-1960. He brought on Engelberg to be Marilyn's primary physician shortly thereafter. Back in 1960, Greenson didn't coordinate with Engelberg regarding prescriptions. Marilyn was taking large amounts of Nembutal when Greenson took over her care from her New York psychiatrist, Dr Kris. He continued prescribing huge amounts of the drug while she was filming *The Misfits*. This is confirmed by both her publicist Rupert Allan and her masseur Ralph Roberts. During a break in the filming Marilyn returned to LA and was hospitalized for exhaustion. In addition to the heat of the desert taking a toll on Marilyn, Greenson also had to confront the fact that the amount of Nembutal Marilyn was taking was getting out of hand. He began prescribing her milder sedatives and chloral hydrate for sleep. Engelberg gave her vitamin shots and injections of B12. Engelberg was apparently unaware that Greenson was experimenting with chloral hydrate, the old and infamous Mickey Finn, knockout drops.

After a brief period of rest, and with a new drug regimen, Marilyn returned to the Nevada desert to resume filming. In Ralph Roberts' unpublished memoirs he tells of how he would pick up the chloral hydrate that Greenson had delivered. He also relates that Marilyn didn't think highly of the drug and that she felt that in the prescribed amounts it wasn't very effective. Apparently she changed her mind when later when she begin to experiment with larger amounts of the chloral hydrate in combination with Nembutal, a potentially lethal combination no doctor would knowingly endorse. After Greenson submitted to her demands for Nembutal he discontinued prescribing chloral hydrate.

Fast forward to spring 1962. Greenson is planning a five week vacation and transfers all responsibility for prescriptions to Engelberg. In addition to barbiturates, Engelberg is prescribing all kings of drugs for Marilyn, including pills for pain and sinus infections, as well as the injections, that now include God knows what. But if we take him at his word he was NOT prescribing chloral hydrate and he didn't think any doctor in the U.S. would.

Let's return to the weekend after Marilyn's birthday. Marilyn is in a bad way. Friday evening, the night of her birthday, she had attended a charity event at Dodgers Stadium. It was a cool and damp evening, and being outside had caused her sinus infection to flare up. She was also despondent. The people she relied on for a support system were not there. Greenson, DiMaggio and Sinatra were all out of the country. DiMaggio had sent a telegram to acknowledge her birthday. Frank sent a gift basket. There's no record that Pat Kennedy Lawford even contacted her. Seemingly desperate for Greenson's return, she contacted his children and when they came over they found her in a bad way.

While Greenson was away he had arranged for a colleague of his, a Dr Milton Wexler to be on-call in case Marilyn needed him. Greenson's kids called Wexler and he came right over. Wexler was an analyst, not a medical doctor, and when he saw the array of prescriptions Marilyn had on hand, he scooped them all into his medical bag before he left. I would say that this was this single most important event that occurred in the summer of 1962. The repercussions of this action by Dr Wexler would lead to the circumstances that played a huge role in Marilyn's death.

I imagine that no single action could freak out an addict more than to see their stash swept up and taken away from them. Is it harsh to call Monroe an addict? Many authors overstate or misunderstand the problem Monroe had with pills. Too often she is portrayed as some kind of party girl, stumbling through her last months, chasing handfuls of pills with copious amounts of booze. That image is harsh and unwarranted. Identifying her addiction as some kind of character flaw is wrong. This often leads fans to deny or downplay her problems with pills. But to deny that Marilyn had become dependent on sleep medication obscures reality and makes any kind of determination of what happened to her difficult.

When Monroe saw her sleep medication taken away, I think it's perfectly understandable that she had a melt down. By evening on Saturday, Marilyn was not only dealing with an ear infection but she was without the meds that helped her sleep. Normally she would turn to Engelberg, but he too was unavailable. In his absence, he had arranged for a Dr Milton Uhley to be on-call. Uhley was summoned and he treated Marilyn from 1AM to 4AM Sunday morning. He gave her medication for the ear infection and some sedatives to help her through the night. But Sunday she was once again left without the medication she had come to rely on.

That's when Pat Newcomb stepped in to help her "friend" out. According to Eunice Murray, "Pat Newcomb moved in for a couple of days to take over Marilyn's care. Pat said she knew just what to do. Presumably, bringing her own sedatives along to let Marilyn use until her doctor returned. The door to her bedroom was closed for two days while Pat kept her sedated."

Newcomb has been described by one biographer as the "ever-present" Pat Newcomb. Truer words were never spoken. Pat Newcomb traveled with Marilyn, went to the studio with Marilyn, shopped with Marilyn, dined with Marilyn, spent evenings and weekends with Marilyn and several people have commented how she isolated Monroe and served as a "buffer" between Marilyn and the outside world. With Greenson gone and Paula Strasberg's influence dwindling, Pat had already moved in to fill the void. With DiMag and Sinatra gone, perhaps Newcomb was filling their void as well. Both Eunice Murray and Marilyn's handyman testify to the fact that Newcomb moved into Marilyn's bedroom that weekend. Murray even claims that Pat slept at the foot of her bed. A coworker of Newcomb's has gone on record saying that rumors of a Newcomb/Monroe affair were circulating at this time and the source of the rumors came from Marilyn's closest circle of friends. These are perhaps baseless rumors, but they do speak to the fact that Newcomb was a constant presence around Monroe and had infiltrated every part of Marilyn's life.

We also learn from Murray that Pat was going around telling everyone that she was Marilyn's best friend. Was she feeling a kind of rivalry with Marilyn's true best female friend, Pat Kennedy Lawford? I think it's fair to ask why had Newcomb inserted herself so prominently in Marilyn's life? Did she feel it necessary to monitor Marilyn's actions? Was she keeping an eye on Marilyn as some authors have suggested? Whatever the reason, it's safe to say that Newcomb was closer to Marilyn than any other person and if anyone knows what Marilyn was up to that last summer it would be her.

It's Monday morning, Marilyn has made it through the weekend. Monroe and Newcomb are still camped out in Marilyn's bedroom. Murray, alarmed at this turn of events, contacts Greenson to inform him about what is going on and to urge his immediate return. It would take several days for him to get back to California and Marilyn is still without the medication she now so desperately needs. Monroe was due back at the studio that morning but as we have seen, Marilyn was holed up with Pat. We are told in some biographies that the reason Marilyn didn't return to work that day was because she felt it was pointless, she knew she was going to be fired, so why bother. Could this be the legitimate reason? Would Fox waste time and money filming Marilyn's scenes if they had already made up their minds to fire her? There's something more going on here. Others say she didn't go back because she was sick. Some biographers allude to her being seen by the studio doctor, Dr Lee Siegel, and that he confirmed Marilyn's sinus infection and recommended that Marilyn stay home. Can this be true? Could Fox not only fire Monroe for this absence, but sue her as well? If their own doctor excused her absence, wouldn't that negate any legitimate basis for a lawsuit?

What is clear is that Marilyn didn't return to work and she was fired because of it. I think it's likely she was sick and had a legitimate reason to not work, however I think something else is going on. Marilyn was without her needed medication, and procuring that medication was her primary concern. I believe that Pat Newcomb, concocted a little scheme to assure Marilyn was never put into a situation were she was without drugs and powerless to do anything about it. Did Newcomb pose as Engelberg's nurse and phone in the prescriptions to the pharmacy?

Fortunately, for people like to me who want to leave no stone unturned in the quest to know what really happened to Marilyn, her fans place considerable value on everything connected to Monroe. That includes the prescriptions and pill bottles she left behind. These occasionally are photographed as they come to auction. As we have seen earlier, an examination of the photos of Marilyn's 1962 prescriptions signed by Dr Engelberg yields an alarming result. Many of the signatures don't match! Starting in this first week of June in 1962, there are a series of prescriptions that look nothing like the prescriptions that include Engelberg's letterhead. Included in this series of bogus looking prescriptions is one for chloral hydrate, the very drug that when combined with Nembutal, resulted in Monroe's death. When you look at the handwriting on these prescriptions it is an almost perfect match to another receipt from the pharmacy it was picked up from. This leads to the question of who called it in to this pharmacy?

This is evidence that should reopen the Marilyn's case. It's evidence that demands explanation. This is all the more true because Dr Engelberg always maintained that he didn't prescribe Marilyn the chloral hydrate and also didn't think any doctor in the US did. He maintained that she must have got the drugs in Mexico., but we know that is not correct.

Someone besides Engelberg phoning the prescription into the pharmacy is a logical solution to the question of how Marilyn got the choral hydrate that killed her. But this solution brings up another vital question. Did anyone help her in this scheme to circumvent doctors and procure drugs illegally? I believe the answer to that question is yes, and the person most likely to have helped Marilyn is the "ever-present" Pat Newcomb.

We know that Murray suspected Newcomb of supplying Monroe with sedatives. Rupert Allan, Marilyn's previous publicist, has gone on record stating he didn't recommend Newcomb because he thought she was a "pill pusher." Greenson, in correspondence with Dr Kris, bemoans the fact that Marilyn has easy access to drugs. One of the reasons Greenson arranged the employment of Eunice Murray was to keep an eye on things, and we know from Newcomb's own testimony that she thought of Murray as a spy. Milton Rudin, Marilyn's lawyer and Greenson's brother-in-law, said Greenson couldn't keep Newcomb and Monroe from exchanging pills.

Did Newcomb also hold the drugs for Marilyn, (away from Murray's prying eyes) and only dole them out to Marilyn as needed? Is there any precedent in Marilyn's life on which to base such a supposition? Yes, there is. Amy Greene, the wife of Marilyn's partner in Marilyn Monroe Productions, tells us that in the mid-fifties, when she was Marilyn's closest female friend, Marilyn asked her to hold her medication and only give her access to what she really needed. Monroe even asked her not to give in when she would demand more. When Monroe was married to Miller he was available to monitor her intake and would lament that there was always another doctor available to help her into oblivion. Marilyn's half sister has told of a visit to New York where the doctor would come by each evening with that night's supply of meds. In the past there was frequently someone to oversee her daily supply of sleeping aids. It's a reasonable assumption, especially given the many close calls Monroe experienced in her final years, that she would ask Newcomb to help her as well. As for Newcomb, if she was half the friend she always portrays herself to be, and if she had even a modicum of concern for her friend, it seems she would want to take precautions so Marilyn didn't accidental overdose.

With all this in mind, a clearer picture of exactly what happened the night Marilyn died begins to emerge. I'm going to go out of my way in this book to provide a theory that gives Ms Newcomb the benefit of the doubt and present a scenario that's an accident.

I suggest that Newcomb, like Greenson, did not know about the Nembutal prescription that Engelberg gave Marilyn on Friday, August 3. Did Newcomb leave a massive dose of chloral hydrate not knowing about the 25 Nembutal? Was her intention just to assure Marilyn was asleep so she could come back and retrieve what RFK had been looking for earlier? Did that plan go terribly wrong? Maybe that's why one of the first things she cried out to Murray when she arrived at Fifth Helena to find Marilyn dead was, "This would have never happened if I was here."

There has always been a question as to whether Marilyn had 50 Nembutal capsules on hand the night she died or 25. The empty pill bottle on the nightstand at the side of her bed was for 25. It was Engelberg's August 3, prescription. But it's claimed she had received another prescription earlier in the week that was also for a quantity of 25. This has lead to a lot of confusion and that confusion has resulted in a vast and persistent over-estimation of the amount of Nembutal she consumed that evening. When estimates of the amount of Nembutal Marilyn had taken that night were made public the early reported amounts (based on newspaper articles) were between the mid-twenties and 47 pills. By far, the 47 number was the most published, and because it was in the headlines, came to be accepted. Was this a chemical analysis based on the amount found in Marilyn's system or a guess based on how many she pills she had on hand? There's reason to believe is was an estimation based on some faulty reasoning, all due to the confusion over this 25 vs 50 issue of the Nembutals. It seems the 50 number was the combination of the two prescriptions of 25 capsules. But one of those was earlier in the week. There is one account in the press that stated Monroe had the Nembutal prescription for three days. The dosage she was instructed to take was one per day. I think this could explain the faulty logic that was used to come up with the number 47. I believe they reasoned: she had a total quantity of 50 within the three days prior to her death. She took one per day. The bottle was found empty, therefore she took 47 on Saturday night. But that's not the way it happened.

Over the years the suggested amount of pills Marilyn took on August 4, 1962 has steadily increased, all on the guess of some "expert." It grew to an inflated amount of 60 something, and most recently, when a well known actor from the Law and Order TV series jumped into the fray with his book, the number of pills thought responsible for the Nembutal in Marilyn's system had ballooned into the nineties. Some recent online estimates come in at over 100! This was all done to "prove" Marilyn didn't die of an oral overdose of drugs, they reason the Nembutal had to be administered by another means, and that points to murder. The exact amount of Nembutal Marilyn took is crucial to understanding how she died. Fortunately, we now have estimates based on science to rely on. Dr Cyril Wecht is perhaps the most well known and respected forensic pathologist in America. He has consulted on many high-profile cases. In his book, *Tales from the Morgue*, he estimates Monroe took 5 chloral hydrates and between 12 and 24 Nembutals. He does say it was likely closer to 24, but even his upper range is lower than almost all previously published estimates.

So with that information established, let's proceed.

It's now mid-June. Marilyn has been fired. Greenson is back and recognizes the need to get Marilyn's drug consumption under control. He coordinates with Engelberg over Marilyn's drug regimen. Greenson gives his recommendations and wants to be notified whenever Engelberg prescribes Marilyn Nembutal, but basically he washes his hands of all responsibility and transfers all drug related duties to Engelberg. Both doctors know Marilyn is very adept at doctor shopping and can find a supply of pills in many places. So as Greenson's wife explained they decided not to say no to her demands, as long as the goal of getting her to reduce her intake was still in effect.

In this scenario (which I will remind the reader is based on conjecture and supposition) neither Greenson or Engelberg are aware that Marilyn is not only self-medicating but, with help from Pat Newcomb, she's self-prescribing. Also, neither

Greenson or Engelberg have any idea she is still using chloral hydrate.

Fast forward to the week before Marilyn's death. By mid-week, Marilyn has got the first prescription of Nembutal (25) and the first chloral hydrate prescription (50). Both of which Newcomb is aware of, holding for Marilyn, and doling out as needed. By Friday, Marilyn has the second chloral hydrate prescription, (in this hypothetical reconstruction Newcomb knows of this prescription) but on that day Monroe gets the second Nembutal (25) prescription from Engelberg, which she doesn't disclose to Newcomb. Marilyn is probably stockpiling. She knows she is going to New York the next week and she probably uses this reasoning to get Engelberg to write the second prescription. Engelberg either forgets to inform Greenson or reasons the information can wait until the next week, when Marilyn had probably promised Engelberg she would be taking the pills.

Using some of the story lines established in Part I and by adding some new ones, we can finally make sense of what happens during Marilyn's last 24 hours. Friday afternoon, before Pat even leaves the office, she has arranged with Marilyn to spend the weekend with her. By this point that was nothing unusual, but on this particular weekend it is imperative that she not only keep an eye on Marilyn, but do her best to talk Marilyn out of her continued attempts to speak with RFK. I believe she also felt it her "mission" to get Marilyn to give the photo that was taken at Cal-Neva back to Peter Lawford so it could be destroyed or delivered to the Kennedys. Rumors of this photo had reached the journalist Dorothy Kilgallen. It's likely Kilgallen had only heard about the photo, as the only ones to see it at this point are Sinatra, Marilyn, Newcomb, Woodfield [the photographer who developed the photo], and Lawford. In this reconstruction Sinatra had given it to Lawford to show Marilyn as a wake up call, not to give it to her. She had snatched it out of his hands and refused to give it back. All this conjecture is based on the premise in Part I that contrary to what Woodfield had always stated, there was at least one photo that escaped destruction. It's also possible all the photos were destroyed and that Marilyn had only heard about the photo but is using this information as a ruse to demand RFK come and speak with her. I maintain in all these scenarios that the fact that Marilyn wanted to speak with Bobby has nothing to do with an affair. This non-existent "affair" has always been the major smokescreen obscuring the real picture of what's going on between the two of them.

Knowing how upset Marilyn was getting, Newcomb was probably giving Marilyn pills on an hour by hour basis, and had been for the past few days. This could explain the tremendous build up of Nembutal in Monroe's liver. Marilyn gets angry with Pat the next morning (Saturday) because she probably felt Newcomb hadn't given her enough meds to sleep through the night (on Friday night Marilyn had to dip into to the secret supply of Nembutal). Greenson arrives in the late afternoon to find Marilyn depressed and angry. He notices upon arrival that Marilyn is showing the effects of being sedated. Is he aware of the Nembutal she was given earlier in the week? If so, then he knows she should have at least a few left so he is reluctant to give her anymore. After a period of observation and consultation he reluctantly gives her a dose of liquid Nembutal that he had brought to calm her down. This could explain the confusion later in the evening when Joe Naar is called and asked to go check on Marilyn. Then a few minutes later he receives another call telling him not to bother because she was probably sleeping, he is told that Greenson had seen her and given her some medication.

Marilyn relies heavily on Greenson for advice and she has told him about Cal-Neva and the photo. He advises her to give the photo to Lawford and let RFK handle things. (This is why in his statements to police he says he advised Marilyn to take a drive to the beach, in other words, to Lawford's house.)

Greenson takes some breaks during the hours he is with Marilyn. During one of those breaks he confers with Murray about spending the night. Newcomb uses that opportunity to slip into see Marilyn.

Knowing Marilyn will be anxious about how she will sleep that night, Newcomb (hypothetically) promises Marilyn she will leave her some chloral hydrate so she can fall asleep that evening. In order to hide it from the snooping eyes of Mrs Murray, Newcomb conspires with Marilyn to dissolve the choral hydrate in a can of coke and leave it in the guest bedroom.

Once Greenson leaves, (Newcomb at this point is gone) Marilyn decides to call it a night. It's been a terrible day and now all she wants to do is sleep. She takes a handful of Nembutal that she has told no one about, and goes to her room to lie down. She gets groggy and starts to fall asleep. She doesn't hear the phone ring when Joe Jr calls, but Mrs Murray rouses her and she grabs one of the Cokes that Mrs Murray had bought earlier, then talks to young DiMaggio. Marilyn is an actress, she is more than capable of putting on a happy face. Marilyn is genuinely excited by the news that Joe's son is not getting married. Between that and the sugar and caffeine rush from the Coke she is now wide awake again. After calling Greenson she decides to go outside and play with Maf.

As the momentarily elation wears off she becomes more and more despondent. She begins to think of the days events. She just wants the day to end and to get some sleep. She returns to the guest bathroom, picking up the secret Nembutal stash and the drug cocktail that Newcomb had left behind. She downs the remaining Nembutal with the Coke laced with chloral hydrate. She retires to her room, telling Mrs Murray on the way that she has decided not to take a ride to the beach.

Was it an accident? Did Marilyn just want to assure that she would fall asleep? I still believe an accident is unlikely and even if it was a deliberate suicide, anyone who helped her in procuring the drugs that killed her would and should be charged with a crime. In this theory the persons intentions were not to kill Marilyn. To turn this into a cold-blooded, premeditated murder, only a few minor adjustments to this scenario are required.

CHAPTER 13

REDRUM: The Murder of Marilyn Monroe

In Steven King's classic movie *The Shining,* viewers see a wall with the word REDRUM flash periodically on the screen throughout the film. Near the end it's revealed that moviegoers had seen the word in a mirror, and what was actually written on the wall was the word MURDER.

History becomes a mirror when we gaze back in time and only see a reflection of things that were happening at the time. To get a clear picture of what is actually going on we have to acknowledge that the reflection of the past we are looking at is distorted. In the days, weeks, then years that followed Monroe's death, we must accept that there was a concerted effort to ignore, downplay and divert attention away from key elements of Marilyn's life. Her connection to the Kennedys, the lesbian rumors, her involvement with the MCA case and the events at Cal-Neva, were effectively covered up for many years. There was one person at the center of this cover-up and if she is responsible for Marilyn's death than she is the one person who had the most to gain from not allowing the true facts get out.

Perhaps all along we've been witnessing Marilyn's death from the wrong vantage point. All theories put forth involve an accident, a suicide or a conspiracy involving an injection, enema or suppository. For numerous reason all these theories can be called into question. Maybe all along it was the work of one person, a person Marilyn trusted, a person that left her a deadly cocktail of drugs. Could it have been a murder that fooled everyone? Did everyone just assume it was an accident or suicide and then go along with a cover-up to hide the fact that the Attorney General had contact with the deceased on the day of her death? I think the actions of almost all the principals involved is best explained by everyone from the doctors, to the police, to the coroner actually believing it was an overdose. Everything that followed was a cover-up to save the reputation of a good, decent man. A man who's reputation could have been harmed, from the embarrassment of an investigation.

It's this cover-up of information and "rush to judgment," that actually did cover up a murder.

If you think there is any credibility to the accidental homicide theory then you can see how easily this can be turned into a murder scenario. To see if it's a possibility we have to have an affirmative answer to one question. Could Marilyn have drank one drink, let's say an amount equal to half a can of soda, that contained the amount of drugs that was found in her system. The answer to that is yes. The smallest number of pills that forensic evidence allows to account for the drug levels found in Monroe's body is 17. This is based on forensic pathologist, Dr Wecht's estimate of 5 chloral hydrate and 12-24 Nembutal. If Marilyn had orally taken 3 or 4 Nembutal before her phone conversation with Joe Jr then the amount of pills in the deadly cocktail could be reduced to 13 or 14. An amount easily hidden in a small amount of liquid.

It's worth noting here that many doctors, for humanitarian reasons, have assisted terminal patients with suicide. In many cases the combination of drugs they use contain barbiturates and chloral hydrate in a drinkable solution. Many of these "death-with-dignity" cocktails contain much more of the same medications that killed Marilyn Monroe. It is possible Marilyn could have consumed this lethal amount of drugs by drinking them. This would explain the empty stomach and the petechial hemorrhage found on the stomach lining. The primary objection to this scenario being a murder would be that it couldn't have been done without her knowledge. But what if she knew the drink contained the drugs, but she was unaware of how much? All you would need for this scenario to be possible is to have someone Marilyn trusted give this to her.

Before we begin to examine if there is anyone that had the means, motive and opportunity to kill Marilyn, let's revisit the seven key areas to see if they can inform this murder scenario.

The Kennedy Connection. This murder scenario requires no sexual relationship between Monroe and any of the Kennedys. I guess you could say the beauty of this scenario is that you don't even have to consider an actual affair between Marilyn and a Kennedy at the time of Monroe's death. The most significant Monroe/Kennedy relationship is Marilyn's bond with Pat Kennedy Lawford, but the most important one on the day she died is the one with Robert Kennedy. The only reason that this platonic relationship becomes important at this time is because rumors of a sexual nature are buzzing in Hollywood, and that buzz has finally made it into print, in newspapers all across the country on August 3, 1962.

Here's Dorothy Kilgallen's column from August 3, 1962: "Marilyn Monroe's health must be improving. She's been attending select Hollywood parties and has become the talk of the town again. In California, they're circulating a photograph of her that certainly isn't as bare as the famous calendar, but is very interesting.... And she's cooking in the sex-appeal department, too; she's proved vastly alluring to a handsome gentleman who is a bigger name than Joe DiMaggio in his hay day. So don't write off Marilyn as finished."

The Lesbian Rumors. The lesbian rumors can largely be disregarded as having anything to do a murder scenario. But they are still important, even if they are wrong. After a detailed examination of these rumors, it's found that their basis (at least around the time of Monroe's death) is probably the result of the "ever-present" Pat Newcomb spending so much time with Marilyn. During the summer of 1962, according to the hearsay evidence that is left to us, Newcomb is the only name connected to these rumors. No affair with Pat Newcomb or anyone else is assumed in this scenario. But the rumors do illuminate just how far Newcomb had inserted herself into every area of Marilyn's life. Fox studio executives wanted Marilyn to get rid of Newcomb. The director of *SGTG* wanted her off the set. Dr Greenson wanted to separate the two, and many of Marilyn's friend's felt that Newcomb had become a barrier they had to go through to even talk to Marilyn. Just how far Monroe had come to rely and trust Newcomb is evident by how Marilyn had her hide in an adjacent room so she could hear the conversation when the executive VP of

Fox came to Monroe's home for a meeting. No one was closer to Marilyn in her final months than Pat Newcomb.

The MCA Case. The MCA case plays a huge role in this scenario. This importance is readily apparent when a timeline of the developments in the case are overlaid onto a calendar of Marilyn's last weeks. Also important is the brief paragraph in Shirley MacLaine's memoir about Marilyn, Bobby and the MCA case. I believe MacLaine's statement clarifies the rumors that were circulating at the time of Marilyn's death. It was not only rumors of an affair, it was rumors that she was using her "boyfriend" to wage some kind of vendetta she had because of her break with MCA. Rumors of this kind could have been disastrous for her career. When Monroe was fired, she fought back not only in the press, but by sending telegrams to all her coworkers who were disadvantaged by cancellation of the film. She wanted them to know it was not her fault and she was ready to get back to work. Less than two weeks before her death, half of Hollywood suddenly found themselves without an agent. July 24, 1962, became known as "Black Tuesday." The headline of the *Daily Variety* that day was "MCA DISSOLVES ENTIRE AGENCY." The government, under RFK's orders, had decreed that the company known around Hollywood as the "black-suited mafia," could not sell off it's talent agency as it had planned. It was just simply gone, as were the agents of some the biggest talent in the industry.

Given the rumors circulating at the time, isn't it reasonable to assume Marilyn would want to tell everyone that the results of the MCA case were not her fault? We know from Ralph Roberts and Rupert Allan that Marilyn was reaching out to her old publicist for something important. Allan was ill and postponed the meeting. George Barris also confirms Marilyn wanted to talk with him about something important. He was out of town and promised to see her the following week. I believe that what see wanted to talk about with them had a lot to do with clearing the air about MCA. The government had decided to go after MCA long before she knew anything about it, I'm sure she wanted that known.

In Shirley MacLaine's *My Lucky Stars: A Hollywood Memoir*, she says: "Marilyn Monroe was unhappy with her agency, MCA, during the time of her relationship with Bobby Kennedy. She went to Kennedy and complained. He commenced proceedings that culminated in the breakup of the most powerful talent agency in town."

About two weeks before Monroe's death, on July 20, 1962, Time magazine ran a story about MCA called, "After the Octopus". Here are excerpts from that article:

"For months Hollywood and Vine has buzzed with gossip of a really big show cranking up in the movie capital. Producer: the U.S. Justice Department... Reluctant villain: the mammoth MCA Inc., which acts as agent for half or more of the U.S.'s top actors, is the nation's largest producer of filmed television shows, leases a library of old movies for late-night...It would be an antitrust epic..."

One week before Marilyn's death, on July 28, 1962, this appeared in Hedda Hopper's column: Hollywood...Studio Workers Hail Return of Zanuck. Workers... Government Attorney Leonard Posner, who insisted MCA give up all its clients, is not popular here. (Source: Chicago Tribune)

Also in this same time period a Hollywood Close-Up editorial by Jaik Rosenstein read: "The attack on MCA is a blow that will set Hollywood back five years... This has all the marks of a deliberate vendetta against MCA, and the Justice Department is moving into an area of which it hasn't the remotest concept... in effect what it has done is to imperil the one organization that has the chance of preserving and maintaining film production in Hollywood..." (Source: The Last Mogul: Lew Wasserman, MCA, and the Hidden History of Hollywood. Dennis McDougal)

In her book, *Mr and Mrs Hollywood: Edie and Lew Wasserman and Their Entertainment Empire,* Kathleen Sharp says this about MCA and the government's case: "In New York, the grand jury made little progress because "witnesses were frightened to death," said one prosecutor. Joseph Cotton had been threatened, Betty Grable had been bribed, and now even investigators were being warned about Werblin and Wasserman, supposed masters of skulduggery. "If you go after [MCA] too hard, watch out for the concrete shoes," one federal attorney was told.

Hollywood's elite assumed that Lew Wasserman was connected to the mob, even though few could explain his ties. But "MCA's connections were an open secret," said Robert Mitchum. "Everyone knew that Stein worked for Al Capone in Chicago. That's how MCA got into the band business. During the Great Depression, Lew worked for Dalitz and his gang, promoting their lavish nightclub, the Mayfair Casino, located in downtown Cleveland."

Cal-Neva Weekend. It took a very long time for information about the Cal-Neva weekend to become public knowledge. Even then that information was grossly distorted. What's almost certain is that photos were taken, photos that included Monroe and Giancana. Six days later a columnist writes about a photo of Marilyn. What's amazing is how few people think these photos are related. If we take Woodfield's word, then Sinatra destroyed all the photos that were taken at Cal-Neva as soon as they were developed. But we have no way of knowing if Sinatra saved a photo or a negative without Woodfield's knowledge. Even if no photo survived, the rumors did. I don't believe Kilgallen ever saw the photo she wrote about in her column, I would bet she only heard about it. If my theory in *Last Love* is correct, this photo is why RFK was at Marilyn's house the day she died, and the photo is what he was looking for. That assumption is not necessary in this workup. For this murder scenario, RFK's presence the day she died is not necessary, nor is an actual photo. What is important is Marilyn's reaction to the circumstances that led to the photo's being taken. She must have been concerned about exactly what and how this was leaked to the columnist, and finally, how to contain the matter from blowing up in the press. These reasons; MCA, Cal-Neva and Kilgallen's column, are why Marilyn is almost desperate to contact RFK on her last weekend alive and demanding to speak to him in person.

RFK's Movie. Robert Kennedy's movie was not only about Hoffa and the teamsters. The movie was based on his book which was about his time fighting the mob with the Rackets Committee. The book mentions Sam Giancana by name as a boss of the Chicago underworld and one of the top hoodlums in the country. There is no way that Monroe didn't know who Giancana was. She knew him as Sinatra's friend, but it's unlikely they ever spent any time together. First, Marilyn and Sinatra's relationship was very private. They seldom appeared together in public even at the height of their relationship. When they were together it was behind closed doors away from prying eyes. When Sinatra spent time with Giancana it was a "boys night out" type of revelry that Marilyn would have never been involved with. Second, she must have known of Giancana's reputation as not only a gangster but a notorious killer as well. She, like Ava Gardner and Lauren Bacall before her, would not have been part of that side of Sinatra's life. So if

Marilyn had ever crossed paths with Giancana while she was in the company of Sinatra, any exchange of words between the two was likely brief, cordial and superficial. Given these facts just imagine how startling it was when Giancana and Rosselli, burst into a room and someone began taking pictures! She must have been outraged and would have demanded to know what Robert Kennedy was going to do about. It should be becoming clear that the reason Monroe was adamant about a face to face with RFK on her last weekend had nothing to do with being dumped.

In addition to this whole mess with Giancana, there is something else that was happening that would have upset and bewildered Marilyn. We've seen how RFK's movie was going to be filmed by Fox studios. It was being produced by Jerry Wald. Wald was a friend of Monroe's and the two had known each other for a decade. Wald had given Marilyn a big break early in her career by including her in the film *Clash By Night*. They had a good working relationship through the years and he always remained on her short list of acceptable directors. It was common knowledge that

Wald had been threatened and harassed by goons trying to intimidate him into not doing the film *The Enemy Within*. Imagine how upset Marilyn must have been when just about three weeks before her death Wald was found dead of mysterious circumstances. I've read almost every biography ever written about Marilyn Monroe and I can't recall one author ever even mentioning Wald's death and Monroe's reaction to it. His death also happened on the same day the Justice Department dropped a bombshell on Hollywood and accused MCA of antitrust law violations. MCA had agreed to sell of it's talent agency and this move was totally unexpected. There is one clue that might show how much these events upset her.

The bill Greenson submitted to the Monroe's estate after her death has been commented on by numerous authors over the decades. The bill details sessions with Marilyn from July 1 through her death. The first half of the bill indicates she saw Greenson nearly every day but always just one session per day. The last half details many days with double sessions.

What was the first day with double sessions? The same day Jerry Wald was found dead and the MCA lawsuit was announced. Wald's death was ultimately reported as a heart attack. But in later years his brother would make a cryptic comment concerning his death. He felt it had something to do with Harry Cohn. Cohn was already dead, but the gangster Cohn hung around with all his life, Johnny Rosselli was alive and well. Rosselli also had known ties to Hoffa, who desperately wanted the film shuttled. And that's exactly what happened.

In the weeks before Marilyn's death Fox changed management. Zanuck had just taken over when thugs came into his office and threatened trouble if the film wasn't canned. That marked the end of Fox's involvement with the film. Imagine how incredulous Marilyn must have been when her studio backed down because of mobster pressure and now Bobby appeared to be doing nothing about what had just happened at Cal-Neva. Marilyn had proven she was not bashful about talking to journalists about the mob. Near the end of her life, during her last trip back to

New York, Marilyn was having a conversation with a British journalist and they were discussing books. Marilyn mentioned that she found the book *The Last Tycoon* to be too romantic in it's portrayal of Hollywood. She said of the author, F. Scott Fitzgerald, "He's missed out on the truly violent gangster element. The mob." It was probably this same trip that Marilyn confided in Paula Strasberg that she was afraid of the mafia. Her fears were not unfounded. Her break with MCA put her in direct opposition to some of the most powerful men in Hollywood. Men with known ties to the mob. Now on the same day it's announced that the Justice Department is pursuing a criminal case against MCA, Wald turns up dead. If Marilyn was anxious and nervous in her last weeks, I think you need look no further than these two facts to explain it.

Marilyn's Publicists. It's only in the last three decades that the term "spin doctor" had become synonymous with press agent or publicist. But even before the term was coined, spinning news was exactly what publicists did. The Merriam Webster definition of spin doctor is: "a person responsible for ensuring that others interpret an event from a particular point of view." In the years that followed Monroe's death that's exactly what Pat Newcomb did, and she was a master at her craft. She learned from, and was mentored by three of the greatest publicists Hollywood ever saw, Henry Rogers, Warren Cohen and Arthur Jacobs. But that was just the beginning. They, along with Pierre Salinger, press secretary to the president, provided what you might call Newcomb's "undergrad" education. She received training for her "masters" degree in propaganda when she joined the United States Information Agency, less than a year after Monroe's death.

You might think that's just my "spin" on what this agency does, but it's not. Fitzhugh Green, author of *American Propaganda Abroad* spent most of his career in the United States Information Agency, and in his book he says that USIA is the "propaganda" arm of the government. For Green this word is roughly synonymous with "psywar" and "public diplomacy." Whatever you call it, this agencies purpose is to put a favorable spin on the presentation of America life and culture to people in foreign countries. Newcomb was taught by the best how to promote a favorable interpretation of events to journalists.

 And that's right what she did from the very beginning. Many people have heard that Newcomb left Hollywood after Marilyn's funeral, was photographed have a good time on the Kennedy yacht in Hyannis Port, and then disappeared to Europe for more than half a year. That's close to what happened. Before her extended "vacation" abroad, she did return to Hollywood for a brief time. How do I know that? For some unknown reason, Hedda Hopper, like Liz Smith after her, was enamored with Ms Newcomb. She showed up in her column all the time. About two weeks after Marilyn's funeral, in her column on August 22, 1962, Hedda Hopper has this to say: "New couple in town – Pat Newcomb and Pierre Salinger." Newcomb did return to town and she came packing a big gun, the president's press secretary. Do you suppose the two of them showing up in town had anything to do with the local press starting to ask questions about the strange circumstances surrounding Marilyn's death? It was also right about this time that Lew Wasserman had made some kind of deal with the Kennedy brothers and the lawsuit against MCA just suddenly went mysteriously and quietly away. How many meetings and dinners with the big wigs of the local press were required to convince the local papers to just bury the connections between Monroe, the Kennedy brothers and the MCA case? History tells us that if that's what they were doing, they were very effective.

But that's not the only example of Newcomb's fingerprints on how the Marilyn story was shaped and molded over the years. On her application to the USIA, under past experience, she said her job for Arthur Jacobs was to "write and plant" press releases. I wonder just how many ideas did she "plant" during interviews with Marilyn's biographers? In 1963, while working for the USIA, it came to her attention that a man named Fred Lawrence Guiles was writing a screenplay for a filmed biography of Marilyn called

Goodbye Norma Jean. Thanks to Newcomb's "help and support" *Norma Jean* became a series of articles published in 1967 in the *Ladies' Home Journal* magazine. These articles became the basis for Guiles' 1969 biography, *Norma Jean: The Life of Marilyn Monroe.* For many years Newcomb had guided this work under the assumption that the relationship of Marilyn to the Kennedys was strictly off limits. However in his book Guiles refers to RFK as the "Easterner with few ties on the coast." He goes on to say this married man who Marilyn was involved with "had come West mainly to work out the details of a film production of a literary property in which he had a hand and to escape the pressures of his work as a lawyer and public servant." He didn't call RFK by name but everyone knew who he was talking about and Newcomb never spoke to him again. She had helped manage the story for many years and was effective in not letting the details of the MCA case or the Cal-Neva weekend become exposed. But all that remained was the Monroe/RFK affair parts, and that's what the conspiracy theorists grabbed on to and they have never let go. Even so, it would take four more years for the average America to take note of the cozy relationship between Marilyn and the Kennedys. It wouldn't come to the public's attention until 1973, when Norman Mailer penned his *Marilyn* biography. Because Mailer brought up the possibility of FBI and CIA, as well as Kennedy involvement in Marilyn's death, he was roundly criticized. Maurice Zolotow, who wrote a 1960 biography of Monroe, publicly chastised Mailer in a six part series that appeared in the Chicago Tribune. Zolotow considers Mailer's work the fourth biography of Marilyn to have been released after Monroe's death. He criticizes Mailer, as well as the other three authors, for not speaking with Greenson, Murray and many of the other principals involved with Monroe on her last day. What's interesting is the one person all the other authors had spoken to. Here's what Zolotow writes in this 1973, Chicago Tribune article: "The curious fact is that except for Pat Newcomb, none of the other principals were interviewed by Mailer, Guiles, Hoyt, or Capell." Curious indeed, only Newcomb was involved in ALL the major biographies of the 60's and early 70's. The "ever-present Pat Newcomb" continued to live up to that moniker.

Not that we've seen how Marilyn's story was shaped in the decade following her death, let's return to the last couple of days of her life. We've seen that Marilyn was trying to contact her old publicist, Rupert Allan the very weekend she died. It's very possible Marilyn was going to talk to the press, and she was going to avoid Pat Newcomb to do it. The one thing, and possibly the only thing that all the conspiracy theorists got right, was that Marilyn had to be silenced. If any person knew how inflammatory Marilyn's comments would be, that person is Pat Newcomb. She had worked with Pierre Salinger researching Dave Beck of the Teamster's union in the very beginnings of the Racket Committee. Many commentators are convinced that she, or her father, is the one who introduced Salinger to Robert Kennedy. Newcomb's father worked for the family of RFK's wife. Newcomb, Salinger and the Kennedys would form close personal and professional bonds, even vacationing together. In her research, Newcomb must have become well aware of the many mob ties in Hollywood. She also new that if certain details were to come out about either the Dave Beck case or the MCA case, it would be very damaging for RFK's career. A man she admired, looked up to, and according to Jeanne Martin, was in love with.

The Prescription Drugs. We've already talked at length about the Nembutal and chloral hydrate. I'd like you now to consider one more drug. The name of this drug is Phenergan. Until recently this drug received little attention and even now I believe it's role in Marilyn's death has gone undetected. Phenergan is commonly prescribed as an antihistamine or as sedative. I believe it was considered just one more sleep aid that was found on Monroe's nightstand at time of her death. The prescription bottle found had been filled on August 3, the same day as Marilyn's last Nembutal prescription. There were 24 of the original 25 pills left in the bottle. Because only one pill was missing I would guess that it wasn't believed by the coroner to be a contributing factor in Monroe's death. I assume that the one pill she did take didn't show up in the autopsy because the toxicologist didn't test for the drug. Why is it important?

If we look back to Monroe's overdose at the Cal-Neva one week previously, we can see that what saved her life that weekend was that she threw up the drugs before she nearly overdosed. Our killer may have realized that this could happen again. Drinking large doses of Nembutal frequently results in vomiting. In doctor assisted suicide with large doses of barbiturates mixed with chloral hydrate, an anti-emetic drug is often required to prevent vomiting. It just so happens that another use of Phenergan is as an anti-emetic. In the Jonestown mass suicides I referenced earlier, Phenergan, in addition to a sedative and chloral hydrate, was included in the Flavor Aid ingredients. These three drugs combine to make a deadly concoction, whose intended use is to kill. Phenergan would be the perfect drug to hide a killers intent, it would be assumed that it was just another sedative, while it helped prevent the subject from throwing up the lethal mixture. The prescription for this drug has found it's way to online auction sites just like the other questionable prescriptions, but this one is unique. First the doctors signature is signed by the same hand that signed the other bogus prescriptions, but the writing of the drug name, dosage and instructions for use are in a completely different handwriting. The prescription paper itself is also different. It looks very similar at first glance to the questionable prescriptions but there are subtle differences. It has a perforated edge and it's clear that it doesn't come from the same prescription pad as the other prescriptions that weren't signed by Engelberg. The date, as previously said is August 3, the same day as Kilgallen's column appeared and the time Marilyn started to make inquiries to locate Rupert Allan. This prescription could be an instrumental piece of evidence in proving premeditated murder.

In American courts, three aspects of a crime must be established before guilt can be established in a murder. They are means, the ability to commit the crime; motive, the reason the defendant committed the crime; and opportunity, whether the defendant had the chance to commit the crime. I'd like to end this chapter by exploring who had the means, motive, and opportunity to commit the crime. Once again, I'd like to remind the reader this is all hypothetical. This scenario is based on assumptions and theories that in the future may be proven to be incorrect. That being said, let's examine the reasons for my belief that Pat Newcomb may have killed Marilyn Monroe.

Means. Only someone close to Marilyn, who she trusted, who saw her on an almost daily basis would have the ability to commit the crime. Pat Newcomb is the only person that meets all of these criteria. She was so close to Marilyn in her last months she surely had to know what was going on with the prescriptions. Newcomb has proven herself to be a smart, maybe even brilliant, capable women who maneuvered her way to the top of her profession. She graduated college with a degree in psychology. This training gave her the ability to read and manipulate people. She would have at least a rudimentary knowledge of medicine and the drugs used by psychiatrists. Dr

Greenson's daughter said that during his house visits to Marilyn he would confiscate pills if he felt that Marilyn had too many drugs on hand. Newcomb herself describes Murray as Greenson's spy. Who else could have held the mystery prescriptions and hid them from both Murray and Greenson? Who saw Marilyn often enough to give her a daily supply of her medication?

Motive. Newcomb's close personal and profession relationship with Robert Kennedy is beyond dispute. Official government files contain notes sent between the two complete with humorous pet names for each other. Her work with Salinger on the Dave Beck research must have filled the heart of this young woman with honor and pride, knowing she helped the man who would become the Attorney General of the United States. A secretary at the Arthur Jacobs agency stated the RFK would frequently call Newcomb, evening trying to reach her that last Saturday. Was Newcomb RFK's eyes and ears in Hollywood? Did she consider herself one of Kennedy's crime-fighters? How far would she go to protect her hero and mentor? What if Kennedy had told her, "Do what you have to do, just make sure Marilyn does not speak to the press about Giancana or the MCA case." Marilyn probably wanted to clear the air about both. Surely she would want to tell Hollywood she was not responsible for a case that could have crippled TV and movie production in LA. Surely she would want to tell her fellow actors that she was not responsible for the turmoil that led to them being without agents. And what if she did go to the press? However minor her role in the case, it was inappropriate. The Justice Department has rules and procedures that need to be followed. Witness's are supposed to come before a grand jury and give their testimony for the record. Marilyn's agent had known about the suit before it became public. He said he knew because Marilyn had told him. As Anthony Summers pointed out in his book, "This is not the way government is supposed to work." RFK was already getting a reputation as being an "end justifies the means" type of operator. Any type of impropriety would have been seized upon and exploited by his enemies. And where would that have led? Any type of metaphoric thread that Marilyn may have pulled by going to the press could have led to a disastrous unraveling. Three months before, keeping a lid on the rumors of an affair with the president had been difficult, now it might be impossible. And what of the Giancana can of worms? What kind of hurricane would that have unleashed. The potential political storm over Giancana's efforts in the election would have been devastating for both RFK and the president. And if the scandal exposed the fact that Giancana was assisting the government in assassination attempts on Fidel Castro, it would have had horrendous implications for the security of the country in an already tense Cold War. There had to be a panic in high places. Newcomb probably didn't know the full gravity of the situation but she knew enough. RFK wouldn't have told her all the facts, but surely he conveyed the sense of urgency involved. So Newcomb knew enough to know that Marilyn couldn't be allowed to go to the press.

One final piece of the puzzle concerning a motive for Marilyn's murder can be found in Gus Russo's book *Supermob*. He relates an anecdote told by Milt Ebbins, Peter Lawfords manager, that Marilyn contacted Sidney Korshak, but for what he didn't know. As we saw earlier Korshak was the Chicago Outfit's "fixer" in LA and Vegas. He was also good friends with Lew Wasserman, president of MCA. Why would Marilyn want to meet with Korshak? Probably the same reasons she wanted to talk with RFK, the Cal-Neva photo and the rumors Kennedy has started the case against MCA on her behalf. This contact with Korshak may be why we have never seen a full copy of Marilyn's August phone calls.

Opportunity. Only someone who was with Marilyn the day she died would have had the chance to kill her. So here's how it went down......allegedly. On Friday, August 3, 1962, Marilyn was receiving encouraging comments about her Life magazine interview that had just hit newsstands. But she was more concerned over an inflammatory Dorothy Kilgallen column that appeared the same day. She was angry, upset, frustrated and eager to set the record straight. For the next two days Lawford and Newcomb spearheaded an effort to calm her down and persuade her from doing something rash. Even her psychiatrist, who must have had some idea the gravity of the situation, was urging her to relax and let it go until things could be sorted out. Marilyn wouldn't let it go and demanded to speak with Bobby immediately. She had already set in motion plans to make a statement about the rumors that RFK was attacking MCA at her urging. She couldn't and wouldn't put the fate of her career once again in the hands of Robert Kennedy. She spent the summer fighting Fox and their lawsuit, now MCA was threatening it's own lawsuit, which is evident from the enormous bill it presented to Marilyn's estate after her death. She was going to speak out. She made plans with her lawyer for Monday and was eager to speak with both Allan and Barris. Barris was already working with Marilyn on a biography, so who better to tell her side of the story. By the end of the day on Friday a decision was made. Marilyn had to be silenced. In this single murderer theory, Newcomb herself would have had to decide the only way to stop Marilyn from ruining everything Bobby had worked for was to have her die from an overdose. It had almost happened the previous last weekend. No one would be suspicious and everyone would assume Marilyn took too many pills. Newcomb probably convinced Marilyn to get another prescription of Nembutal from Engelberg by reminding her they were going out of town the next week and she would need a supply of medicine. Marilyn probably used the same logic on a distracted Engelberg to get him to give her another prescription. In addition to the Nembutal, another prescription was obtained that day, the one for Phenergan. Newcomb made sure she manipulated an invitation out of Marilyn to spend the night. She still probably hoped to get Marilyn to change her mind, but until that happened, she wasn't going to let her out of her sight.

  Saturday provided one last opportunity for Newcomb to talk Marilyn out of going public, but the discussions broke down, and turned into an argument. Events at the house that day left Newcomb no other options. She had to do something drastic. Greenson arrived to calm Marilyn down. Since Murray had been around all day, Newcomb was probably already holding Marilyn's prescriptions in her overnight bag. If she had just left when Greenson arrived, Marilyn might have panicked watching her pills leave with her. Newcomb was forced to stay. When it became clear that Murray was going to spend the night she had to improvise. She waited until Greenson took a break from Marilyn to confer with Murray. While Greenson and Murray spoke, she then slipped into Marilyn's bedroom with a can of soda and one Phenergan. She knew she didn't have much time. She handed the pill to Marilyn and gave her the can to wash it down, telling her it was a new sedative she had just purchased. She then took the can from Marilyn and told her she was going to leave soon. She explained a plan that would ensure Greenson didn't discover and confiscate her meds. She would hide the meds from Greenson and Murray by dissolving Marilyn's night time dose in the can. Marilyn hadn't sleep well Friday night and it had become an issue on

Saturday. Maybe she felt Pat hadn't given her enough meds the night before to get the job done. Newcomb probably had to assure Marilyn there would be enough meds mixed with the pop to insure she would sleep. Marilyn may have been unconvinced and asked Newcomb to also leave the remaining Nembutal. Later, when she couldn't find these she called and asked Greenson if he took them.

Mixing barbiturates and chloral hydrate into a liquid was nothing new for Marilyn. The executive vice president of Fox studio had witnessed her do it with champagne in his presence. It was the perfect plan. Newcomb would only have to be one of the first people on the scene after Marilyn was discovered, so during the resulting confusion she could get the prescription bottles back into the house. Natalie Trundy, who would later marry Arthur Jacobs, said Newcomb had told her that she was the first on the scene after Marilyn's death.

Newcomb told Marilyn she would leave the can in the phone room. Since Murray wasn't much of a housekeeper she knew it would still be there in the evening. Before Greenson returned to the bedroom, Newcomb slipped out and into the guest bathroom, where she could mix the deadly cocktail undetected. Greenson had wanted Newcomb to leave, and now that Marilyn was sure she'd have her nightly meds, she let Greenson send her away. Greenson noticed the sedatives effects on Marilyn, but he may have given her a few Nembutal before he left. Marilyn had probably taken these and become drowsy before her conversation with Joe Jr. The excitement from the call reinvigorated her. She went outside for a game of catch with Maf.

Afterward she decided to turn in for the night. She entered the phone room, picked up the can and took it into the bathroom. While looking in the mirror she swirled the contents to make sure nothing had settled and it was well mixed. She drank the deadly cocktail down. The taste was bitter and she knew it was strong. Stronger than anything she had ever mixed herself. Knowing it was strong might have been a relief. At least now she would be able to sleep. When she finished drinking the lethal mix she threw the can into the wastebasket. Like almost every other night she grabbed the phone with the intent to makes some calls until the pills took effect. She left the phone room and walked towards her bedroom, stopping only long enough to wish Mrs Murray, "Good night."

Made in the USA
Lexington, KY
15 February 2019